Macmill
Series E

Advance
Advance
Applied
Asset V
Building
Building
Building
Building
Building
Building
Building
Building
Civil E
   Ivor
Civil E
Civil E
Comme
   Eric
Compu
Conflic
Constr
   A.C.
Constr
Consti
Contra
Contra
Cost
Design
Development Site Evaluation   N.P. Taylor
Environmental Management in Construction Alan Griffith
Environmental Science in Building, third edition   R. McMullan
European Construction – Procedures and Techniques B. Cooke
   and G. Walker
Facilities Management – An Explanation Alan Park
Greener Buildings – Environmental Impact of Property   Stuart Johnson
Housing Associations Helen Cope
Housing Management – Changing Practice Christine Davies (Editor)
Information and Technology Applications in Commercial Property
   Rosemary Feenan and Tim Dixon (Editors)
Introduction to Building Services, second edition   Christopher A. Howard
   and Eric F. Curd
Introduction to Valuation, third edition   D. Richmond

Marketing and Property People Owen Bevan

Principles of Property Investment and Pricing, second edition W.D. Fraser

Project Management and Control David Day

Property Finance David Isaac

Property Valuation Techniques David Isaac and Terry Steley

Public Works Engineering Ivor H. Seeley

Resource Management for Construction M.R. Canter

Quality Assurance in Building Alan Griffith

Quantity Surveying Practice Ivor H. Seeley

Recreation Planning and Development Neil Ravenscroft

Resource and Cost Control in Building Mike Canter

Small Building Works Management Alan Griffith

Structural Detailing, second edition P. Newton

Sub-Contracting under the JCT Standard Forms of Building Contract
  Jennie Price

Urban Land Economics and Public Policy, fifth edition Paul N. Balchin,
  Gregory H. Bull and Jeffrey L. Kieve

Urban Renewal – Theory and Practice Chris Couch

1980 JCT Standard Form of Building Contract, second edition
  R.F. Fellows

Series Standing Order
If you would like to receive future titles in this series as they are published, you can
make use of our standing order facility. To place a standing order please contact your
bookseller or, in case of difficulty, write to us at the address below with your name
and address and the name of the series. Please state with which title you wish to begin
your standing order. (If you live outside the United Kingdom we may not have the
rights for your area, in which case we will forward your order to the publisher concerned.)

Customer Services Department, Macmillan Distribution Ltd
Houndmills, Basingstoke, Hampshire, RG21 2XS, England.

Introduction to Valuation

Third Edition

David Richmond

Principal Lecturer
Department of Surveying
Nottingham Trent University
Nottingham

MACMILLAN

First edition 1975
Reprinted five times
Second edition 1985
Reprinted twice
Third edition 1994

Published by
MACMILLAN PRESS LTD
Houndmills, Basingstoke, Hampshire RG21 2XS
and London
Companies and representatives
throughout the world

ISBN 0-333-61484-4

A catalogue record for this book is available
from the British Library.

10	9	8	7	6	5	4	3	2	1
03	02	01	00	99	98	97	96	95	94

Printed in Great Britain by
Mackays of Chatham PLC, Chatham, Kent

David would like to dedicate this book to the memory of his parents, Samuel and Susan Richmond

Contents

Preface to the First Edition   xi

Preface to the Second Edition   xii

Preface to the Third Edition   xiii

1 The Concept of Valuation   1
  1.1 The Surveying Profession   1
  1.2 The Function of the Valuer   1
    1.2.1 The Purchase and Sale of Property   2
    1.2.2 The Letting of Property   3
    1.2.3 Valuation for Loan Purposes   3
    1.2.4 Rating, Insurance, Taxation and Other
        Specialised Purposes   4
  1.3 Factors Affecting the Value of Property   4
  1.4 Marketing of Property   7
  1.5 The Purpose of Valuation Tables   7

2 Principles and Sources of Investment   9
  2.1 The Investment Market   10
  2.2 Sources of Investment   10
    2.2.1 Banks and Building Societies   11
    2.2.2 Stocks and Shares   11
    2.2.3 Unit Trusts   13
    2.2.4 Land and property   13
  2.3 Yield and Dividend   13

3 Land and Property as an Investment   15
  3.1 Legal Estates   15
    3.1.1 Equitable Interests   17
  3.2 Controls on Land Usage   18

3.2.1 Private Control   18
3.3 Statutory Controls   20
3.3.1 Planning Control   20
3.3.2 Building and Other Controls   22
3.4 Characteristics of Land and Property   24
3.4.1 External Influences   24
3.4.2 Deterioration of the Structure   25
3.4.3 Changes in Taste and Demand   25
3.4.4 Effect of Adjacent Activities   26
3.4.5 Economic Activities   26
3.4.6 Changes in Legislation   26
3.4.7 Inflation   27
3.4.8 Relationship to Other Investment Sources   28
3.4.9 Costs of Transactions   28
3.5 Determination of Rental Value   28
3.6 Rent and Capital Value   31
3.7 Outgoings   31
3.7.1 Rent Payable to a Superior Landlord   32
3.7.2 Repairs   32
3.7.3 Insurances   33
3.7.4 Management   34
3.7.5 Landlord's Services   34
3.7.6 Bad Debts and Voids   35
3.7.7 Rent Charges   35
3.7.8 Property Taxes and Charges   36
3.8 Characteristics of Different Types of, and Interests
in, Property   36
3.8.1 Ground Rents   36
3.8.2 Agricultural Land   37
3.8.3 Residential Properties   38
3.8.4 Shops   39
3.8.5 Offices   40
3.8.6 Industrial Premises   41
3.8.7 Other Types of Property   41
3.9 Patterns of Yields   42

4 The Mathematics of Valuation   43
4.1 Arithmetical Progressions   43
4.2 Geometrical Progressions   45
4.3 Simple Interest   47
4.4 Compound Interest   50
4.5 Mortgage Repayments   52
4.6 Depreciation   54

5 Construction and Analysis of Valuation Tables   57
  5.1 Single Rate Tables   58
      5.1.1 Amount of £1 (A)   58
      5.1.2 Present Value of £1 (PV)   60
      5.1.3 The Amount of £1 per annum   61
      5.1.4 Annual Sinking Fund (s)   63
      5.1.5 Years' Purchase (YP) or Present Value of
            £1 per annum   65
      5.1.6 Years' Purchase in Perpetuity (YP)   67
      5.1.7 Years' Purchase of a Reversion to a Perpetuity   68
      5.1.8 Interest at Intervals of Less Than One Year   70
      5.1.9 Income to be Received at Intervals of More
            Than One Year   71
  5.2 Dual Rate Tables   73
      5.2.1 Years' Purchase or Present Value of
            £1 per annum (YP)   73
      5.2.2 The Effect of Tax on the Sinking Fund
            Element of the Dual Rate YP   77
      5.2.3 The Annuity £1 will Purchase   80
  5.3 Internal Rate of Return Tables   81
  5.4 Mortgage Instalment Table   82
  5.5 Valuation Formulae and Their Inter-relationship   84
  5.6 Adjustment of Formulae for Incomes Other Than
      Annually in Arrears   94

6 Discounted Cash Flow Techniques   99
  6.1 Net Present Value   99
  6.2 Internal Rate of Return   100
      6.2.1 Internal Rate of Return Tables   103

7 The Valuation of Freehold and Leasehold Interests   107
  7.1 Freehold Interests   107
      7.1.1 Perpetual Income   108
      7.1.2 Varying and Deferred Incomes   109
      7.1.3 Hardcore or Layer Method   114
  7.2 Leasehold Interests   116
      7.2.1 Fixed Income for the Period of the Lease   117
      7.2.2 Varying and Deferred Incomes During the
            Period of the Lease   118
      7.2.3 Non-Tax-Paying Investors   120
  7.3 Profit Rent   122
  7.4 Errors in Multi-Stage Leasehold Valuations   124
      7.4.1 Double Sinking Fund Method   126

7.4.2 Pannell's Method 127
7.4.3 Sinking Fund Method 128
7.5 Premiums 129
7.5.1 Calculation of the Premium or Reduction
in Rent 130
7.6 Combined Freehold and Leasehold Valuations 132
7.7 Purchasers with a Special Interest 137

8 Methods of Valuation **145**
8.1 The Investment Method 145
8.2 The Comparison Method 145
8.3 The Residual Method 149
8.4 The Profits or Accounts Method 151
8.5 The Reinstatement Method 152
8.6 The Contractor's Method 153

9 Inflation and Growth **157**
9.1.1 Valuation Methods 157
9.1.2 Constant Rent 160
9.1.3 Bibliography 161

10 Computer Applications **163**
10.1 Definitions and Terminology 163
10.1.1 The Machine 163
10.1.2 The Program 164
10.1.3 Data 164
10.1.4 Processing 164
10.1.5 Output 164
10.2 Computer Hardware 164
10.3 Computer Software 165
10.3.1 Programming Languages 165
10.3.2 Operating Software 165
10.3.3 Applications Software 166
10.4 The Property Professional and Computer
Applications 167
10.5 Property Valuation and Appraisal and Computer
Spreadsheets 167
10.5.1 Background and Nature of a Spreadsheet 167
10.5.2 Using a Spreadsheet 168
10.6 Example of Residual Valuation Spreadsheet 170
10.7 References 172

Answers to Questions 175

Index 223

Preface to the First Edition

The main purpose of this book is to assist those studying the subject of valuation for the Part 1 Examination of the Royal Institution of Chartered Surveyors and other relevant professional bodies, and for degrees and diplomas in estate management at universities and polytechnics. I also hope that it will be helpful to quantity, building and mineral surveying students, who require a knowledge of valuation in their studies, and others interested in the principles and techniques of property valuation.

Most examinations in valuation contain a number of questions involving calculations. In this connection the reader may benefit from attempting the questions included in Chapters 3, 6, 7 and 8, the answers being provided at the end of the book. The chapter on mathematical aids should be of value for purposes of revision.

When answering questions with tax implications, the reader should apply the tax rates current at the time. I have used different tax rates throughout the book, so that the reader will appreciate that tax rates can vary according to the differing financial and personal circumstances of investors, and Finance Act changes.

I would like to express my thanks to Dr I.H. Seeley for his invaluable advice and encouragement; also to many other colleagues at Trent Polytechnic for their helpful comments.

Sincere thanks are also due to the Royal Institution of Chartered Surveyors and the Universities of London and Reading for permission to use past examination questions as examples and test questions.

Nottingham
Spring 1975

DAVID RICHMOND

Preface to the Second Edition

It is nine years since the First Edition of this book appeared, and during that time there have been considerable developments in valuation techniques and research.

In this edition I have taken out my original chapter on mathematical aids, due to the widespread use of calculators. I have updated the main text and extended Chapter 5 (originally Chapter 6) to take account of payments receivable other than annually in arrears.

Two new chapters have been produced on discounted cash flows and allowing for inflation and growth.

I have received helpful comments both from my students and my colleagues at Trent Polytechnic, for which I am very grateful. I would especially like to thank my 'partner' in valuation teaching, Neil Crosby, for his assistance in the preparation of Chapter 9.

I would also like to thank Professor Ivor H. Seeley, the Series Editor, for his continued encouragement and assistance.

In the preface to the First Edition, I omitted to thank my mother for her help with proof-reading and indexing. I can now rectify this and thank her, rather belatedly!

Nottingham　　　　　　　　　　　　　　　　　　DAVID RICHMOND
Spring 1984

Preface to the Third Edition

Since the Second Edition of this book was produced, the property market has suffered from the effects of a world-wide recession, which has had an influence on the pattern of yields and rents obtainable from property. I have, therefore, revised and provided new calculations and also updated the text.

Additional material has been incorporated on the Hardcore or Layer Method, Errors in Multi-Stage Leasehold Valuations and Purchasers with a Special Interest.

A new chapter has been produced on Computer Applications, and I am greatly indebted to Steven B. Tyler, my colleague at the Nottingham Trent University, for writing this chapter and also for his helpful comments.

I would also like to thank Professor Ivor H. Seeley, the Series Editor, for his continued support over many years, and Diane R. Butler for her encouragement and friendship.

I am grateful for the assistance of Andrew J. Buckley and Graham S. Parkinson, currently students at the Nottingham Trent University, for undertaking the unenviable task of checking my calculations.

Lastly, sincere thanks to Adam Fidler for typing the amendments and additions – quite an achievement for a 15-year-old!

Nottingham   DAVID RICHMOND
Autumn 1993

1 The Concept of Valuation

1.1 THE SURVEYING PROFESSION

Surveyors will be employed whenever activities involve land, construction or property. They may be members of the Royal Institution of Chartered Surveyors and/or the Incorporated Society of Valuers and Auctioneers. *and previously the Incorporated Society of Valuers and Auctioneers*

The Royal Institution of Chartered Surveyors has seven sectors, namely:

(1) *Land and Hydrographic* – the work involves the collection, management and presentation of accurate measurements of the earth's surface, its features, building and boundaries of its rivers and oceans.
(2) *Minerals* – this involves activities relating to the extraction of minerals, problems on landfill and related issues.
(3) *Rural Practice* – activities in this sector will include management, development, marketing and valuation of all rural property, including country estates, farms and livestock.
(4) *Building Surveying* – advice will be given to owners and occupiers on the economic, legal, technical, structural and design aspects of their buildings, on their potential for extension and refurbishment and on cost-effective maintenance.
(5) *Quantity Surveying* – this requires expertise on the cost and management of all construction projects, whether building, civil or heavy engineering.
(6) *Planning and Development* – this work involves a detailed knowledge of planning law, assessing and advising on the best use of the available resources of land and buildings.
(7) *General Practice* – this involves the valuation, marketing and management of all types of residential, commercial and industrial property for occupation or investment. The valuer is a member of this sector.

1

1.2   THE FUNCTION OF THE VALUER

The valuer is primarily concerned with the valuation of land and/or buildings. Valuation may be defined as the estimation of the capital or rental value of land and/or buildings at a certain time. The valuer may also practise in estate agency, land economy, town and country planning or urban estate management.

An *estate agent* negotiates on behalf of clients the purchase, sale or leasing of property; he may also arrange for the borrowing of capital by mortgage and advise on market and rental values of property. A *land economist* appraises the economic consequences of the use or development of land, taking into account financial and planning considerations. In *town and country planning*, the surveyor advises on all forms of land use and the economic problems and consequences involved with planning and development. The *urban estate manager* manages residential, commercial and industrial properties on behalf of the owners.

The valuer's special expertise, however, is to assess the capital or rental value of any particular property at a certain time. He will need to know the purpose for which the valuation is required and the intentions and circumstances of the client or employer on whose behalf it is being prepared. This information is essential, because it will affect the calculation of value. The valuation may be required for any of the following purposes.

1.2.1   The Purchase and Sale of Property

The valuer may represent either the prospective purchaser or the vendor. The price at which property is bought and sold may be established by private negotiation, tender or auction. The valuer representing the vendor may advertise that a property is for sale at a certain price and invite offers for its purchase. He will then negotiate with the prospective purchaser, who is the person to submit the most acceptable offer. The valuer may recommend the price at which the property should be offered.

Alternatively, property may be sold by tender; the vendor's valuer invites written offers to be submitted by a certain date. The vendor may then negotiate with the prospective purchaser, who is the person to submit the highest price.

A third method is to sell property by auction. The property is advertised for sale at a certain place and time. Bids for the purchase of the property are invited, and the offer by the bidder of the highest price may be accepted. However, prior to auction, a reserve price may be fixed, that is, a price below which the property will not be sold.

The valuer who represents the vendor may recommend which method would be the most appropriate. He may take into account local and national circumstances. For example, a residential property may attract prospective purchasers from within the immediate locality only; however, there may be considerable local demand for this type of property, and the valuer may recommend a sale by private negotiation. Alternatively, he may feel that the demand would justify an auction sale. A commercial property having attractive investment possibilities may appeal to investors on a national scale, and the valuer may recommend sale by auction or tender.

1.2.2 The Letting of Property

The valuer may represent the owner of property – the landlord – who wishes to let it for the receipt of an annual sum (rent) or he may represent the tenant, who wishes to occupy the property for the payment of rent. In either case, the valuer may recommend to his client a price, which he considers to be the annual rental value of the property. He may also negotiate on behalf of his client the terms of the lease or tenancy agreement. If a landlord and tenant cannot agree the rent to be paid for the occupation of property, an independent valuer may be appointed to assess the rental value.

Leases of commercial property will provide for regular rent reviews, and there will also be the opportunity to renew leases on their expiration for further periods of time. The machinery for dealing with the renewal of a lease is governed by legislation such as the Landlord and Tenant Act 1954 and the Law of Property Act 1969. In these situations, it may be necessary to assess current market rental value which will be influenced by factors such as: floor area measurement (very necessary to know whether gross or net floor areas have been adopted and whether dimensions should be taken internally or externally); rent review patterns; repairing obligations; rebuilding clauses; tenants' improvements; restrictive covenants (refer to Chapter 3), and rates and service charges.

1.2.3 Valuation for Loan Purposes

Banks, building societies, insurance companies and any other lending institution, when involved in either short- or long-term finance (such as for mortgage purposes), will require an independent valuation of the property, which is their security. This will enable them to assess the degree of risk that may be involved. If the valuation is for a commercial mortgage or development funding, the valuer will give an opinion on the value at present and assess the potential that is offered, i.e. the marketability, growth prospects and investment yields. Mortgages are dealt with in Chapters 4 and 5.

1.2.4 Rating, Insurance, Taxation and other Specialised Purposes

The valuer may assess the value of property for specialised purposes such as rating assessment, payment of Inheritance Tax, taxation liabilities, insurance purposes and its inclusion in company accounts.

The valuer may be employed in private practice, public service or be engaged on company work. The valuer employed in private practice with a professional firm may offer a service to all types of clients. The public service valuer may be employed by a government department, a nationalised industry or local government. The valuer engaged on company work may be employed by a property company, industrial or insurance group, or building society.

1.3 FACTORS AFFECTING THE VALUE OF PROPERTY

The value of an interest in property may be defined as the amount of money which can be obtained for that interest at a particular time from those who are able and willing to purchase it.

The definition of value has caused much debate and the Assets Valuation Standards Committee of the Royal Institution of Chartered Surveyors redefined 'Open Market Value' as from 1 June 1992 to mean

The best price at which the sale of an interest in property might reasonably be expected to have been completed unconditionally for cash consideration on the date of valuation, assuming: (a) a willing seller; (b) that, prior to the date of valuation, there had been a reasonable period (having regard to the nature of the property and the state of the market) for the proper marketing of the interest, for the agreement of price and terms and for the completion of the sale; (c) that the state of the market, level of values and other circumstances were, on any earlier assumed date of exchange of contracts, the same as on the date of valuation; (d) that no account is taken of any additional bid by a purchaser with a special interest, and (e) that the property will continue to be owner-occupied, or let by a public or other body pursuant to delivery of a service, for the existing use. (Statements of Asset Valuation Practice and Guidance Notes – RICS, 3rd Edition, 1990)

This definition assumes that a reasonable marketing period has taken place before the valuation date which coincides with the date of completion of the sale.

Valuations relating to purchasers with a special interest will be dealt with in Chapter 7.

A purchaser of an interest (legal estate) in property may buy for occupation, investment or speculation. Legal estates are considered in Chapter 3. A purchaser for personal occupation will have regard to location and social and commercial facilities. In many instances the property will only attract a local market. A purchaser for invest-ment purposes will consider the return he can obtain from the prop-erty in the form of rent, security and capital growth. (The calculations of value in this book are primarily for investment situations.) High-class investments frequently attract prospective purchasers on a na-tional scale.

Speculators may purchase property with the hope of selling at a higher price in the future, thus making a capital gain. This type of activity may be curtailed by external restraints such as Income Tax and Capital Gains Tax liabilities.

In some transactions purchase of property may be for both occu-pation and investment. A prospective purchaser for investment pur-poses may compare property with other types of investment such as stocks and shares; these are considered in Chapter 2. The valuer, when ascertaining value, must be aware of the economic and legal factors which affect both the existing and potential use of land and buildings; these are discussed in Chapters 2 and 3.

Land is unique as an investment because it is naturally limited in supply. If there is considerable demand for manufactured products, the demand may be met by increasing the supply of these products. This is not so in the case of land, and it may be impractical to create additional land by schemes such as reclamation from the sea. If the supply of land cannot meet the demand for it, this will be reflected by increases in price.

The supply of land available for particular uses such as residential and commercial development is limited not only by natural factors, such as location, topography and the load-bearing capacity of the ground, but also by private and statutory factors. An owner of land or property may be restricted from using the land or property exactly as he wishes. This may be because, at some time in the past, a condition has been imposed restricting the use of land or property, and it is still legally binding at the present time. Statutory control may, however, have a greater influence on the eventual use of land than private control. It is essential that, when the demand for land is increasing due to population growth and improved living and technological standards, its eventual use should benefit as many people as possible. Successive governments have introduced legislation relating to the use and development of land and buildings in an attempt to make the best possible use of the land available.

Perhaps the most effective legislation is that relating to planning control, which is considered in detail in Chapter 3. The local government authority dealing with planning (the local planning authority) has power to allocate the land in its administrative area for particular uses such as agricultural, residential or commercial. The authority also has the power to require an owner of land or buildings, who wishes to develop or change the use of that land or building, to obtain planning permission. An example will illustrate how these powers operate. An owner of land wishes to build a factory upon land, and applies for planning permission. The land is allocated for residential development so the authority would normally refuse permission for industrial development but permit residential development.

The value of land for residential development would normally be different from that for industrial development, so that the type of planning permission granted has a significant effect upon land value.

For several years, the government has been concerned that certain investors and speculators have enjoyed considerable financial benefits from the disposal of property and the sale or renting of new developments. An attempt has been made to reduce these benefits by requiring the investor or speculator to pay Income Tax, Capital Gains Tax or Development Land Tax (now abolished) assessed on his gain. The rates at which taxes are paid may be altered according to economic circumstances. It is essential that the valuer knows the current tax rates when preparing a valuation.

The aim of the valuer is to assess market or rental value of property at a particular time, taking into account the factors previously discussed. Different valuers may, however, produce different values. They may have based their estimate of valuation upon prices obtained from similar transactions, and perhaps adjusted these values to take account of differences in the property. In many cases, these differences of opinion between valuers may be easily resolved by discussion or negotiation. However, in times of unstable market conditions, the valuer's task is made more difficult. Because the market value is dependent upon income to be received in the future, the valuer must attempt to anticipate future economic trends, which will require considerable skill and knowledge.

Valuation work also requires a certain amount of mathematical skill and the ability to set out calculations of value in a logical and comprehensible manner. The valuer may be required to justify his valuation to the Lands Tribunal (which consists of valuers and lawyers who are appointed to settle disputes relating to land and property), and local valuation court or other judicial and quasi-judicial proceedings.

1.4   MARKETING OF PROPERTY

The valuer has the responsibility of obtaining the best possible deal for the client and this will involve skilful marketing of the property, whether it be for sale or leasing.

This will involve the preparation of detailed particulars and photographs for newspaper advertising, window displays and handout material.

The valuer must comply with the Property Misdescriptions Act 1991, which requires that particulars are not false or misleading; this applies not only to written particulars but also to oral statements and photographs. Misdescription may lead to a substantial fine or, ultimately, a banning order under the instruction of the Director-General of Fair Trading.

1.5   THE PURPOSE OF VALUATION TABLES

To ascertain value, the valuer will need to possess certain numerical information such as the annual rent obtainable from the property and the return per annum which a purchaser could expect. This may be used mathematically to arrive at a figure of estimated value.

Example. Your client wishes to purchase a shop, which produces an annual income of £10 000. Similar properties have recently yielded returns of 8 per cent per annum. Estimate the value of the property.

£10 000 is 8 per cent of the capital value, hence

the capital value = £10 000 × 100/8

$$= £10\,000 \times 12.5$$

$$= £125\,000$$

The multiplier of 12.5 is termed the 'Years' Purchase' (YP).

The above example assumes that the annual income is perpetual. Many calculations will involve income which is receivable for limited periods only, and these calculations may be complex. The use of valuation tables saves time and may reduce mathematical error. There are several different types of valuation table. Their construction is considered in Chapter 5 and their application to the calculation of values in Chapters 6, 7 and 8. The appropriate tables used in valuation are contained in *Parry's Valuation and Investment Tables* (Estates Gazette Limited, 1989). In recent years, there have been other tables produced giving further information – P. Marshall, *Donaldsons Investment Table* (Donaldsons, 1979); J.J. Rose, *Rose's Property Valuation Tables* (The Freeland Press, 1977) and P. Bowcock, *Property Valuation Tables* (Macmillan, 1978).

2 Principles and Sources of Investment

The essential nature of any investment is the forgoing of a capital sum in return for a regular income over a period of time. A person who has capital surplus to his immediate requirements may retain this for future contingencies. However, a better alternative would be to put his capital to work by investing it and enjoying a return of income, probably on an annual basis.

The prudent investor will consider the alternative types of investment available to him by comparing each with the 'ideal investment'. This has four qualities:

(1) Security of capital in relation to ease of withdrawal. The investor may, at some future date, need to transfer his investment back into cash at short notice. It is thus essential that the investment can be sold for, or converted to, cash at any particular time.
(2) Security of income in relation to purchasing power. The investor will wish to ensure that the regular or annual income can be maintained in the future. He would also hope that the income would increase sufficiently in the future to counteract inflationary trends.
(3) Minimum inconvenience and expense in management. Investments may vary in the amount of inconvenience and cost of collecting or obtaining the income.
(4) Minimum of inconvenience and expense in selling. Investments in banks and building societies may be easily and cheaply converted into cash, whereas conversion of those in land and property will prove to be more costly and time-consuming.

The investor will also consider the yield given by each of his alternative investment outlets. The yield is the relationship between the capital paid for the investment and the income which derives from it.

9

Example. A man invests £1000 in a deposit account in a bank. His annual interest or return is £90. The yield is 90/1000 × 100 = 9 per cent.

If the ideal investment with the four desirable qualities did exist, the investor would merely require a fee for the use of his money. In practice, however, investments will differ in the extent to which they possess these four qualities, and these differences will cause a varying pattern of yields. If one investment appears to involve greater risk than another, then the investor will expect a greater return or reward. Hence, the lower the ratio of risk to capital and income, the smaller will be the yield.

2.1 THE INVESTMENT MARKET

Some holders of surplus cash will purchase investments, and at any given time there will be a stock of investments in existence. Some investors may wish to turn their investments back into cash and, conversely, some holding cash may wish to invest it.

The function of the investment market is to equate these two opposing activities. If the supply of an investment at a particular time is greater than the demand for it at the prevailing price, then the price will fall and the yield will rise in consequence. This will probably stimulate increased demand, because of the improved yield. It might also have the effect of reducing the supply of investments available for purchase because the lower price would deter existing owners of those investments from selling. This process would continue until supply and demand became equal. At a time of economic uncertainty, there may be a tendency to retain surplus capital rather than invest it. This may result in depressed prices and enhanced interest rates. The level of interest rates will also be influenced by the Minimum Lending Rate (formerly the Bank Rate) operated by the Bank of England and the European Union.

2.2 SOURCES OF INVESTMENT

The investor may have a number of alternative sources available to him, such as

(1) Banks and Building Societies
(2) Stocks and Shares
(3) Unit Trusts
(4) Land and Property

2.2.1 Banks and Building Societies

Investment in the deposit account of a bank will compare favourably with the ideal investment since invested capital is quickly and cheaply recouped if required. The income (interest) is safe and is added to the invested amount at regular intervals. The sum of a bank's capital investments will influence the amount that it will be able to lend. Lending may take the form of either an overdraft or a personal loan. An overdraft is not a personal right and it must be adequately backed with security for the loan required. The security must have a greater value than the amount to be borrowed, and banks favour securities such as property and stocks and shares which can be readily realised.

A personal loan does not require security and could be regarded as an alternative to hire purchase. A sum is borrowed for a specific purpose on the basis of monthly repayments with interest, this interest being paid on the original loan and not the declining balance owed.

Building societies have many of the desirable qualities attributable to investments with the banks. Both capital and income are secure, and the building society attempts to cater for a wide range of investors. Sums may be deposited by an investor at any time, although the regular saver may undertake to invest an agreed amount at fixed intervals, often monthly, and in return the building society pays a higher rate of interest.

The availability of capital for borrowers is directly influenced by the total amount of investment in the building society. The lending of capital is normally undertaken by means of a mortgage. The building society will need to consider the age, personal circumstances and earning capacity of prospective borrowers, in order to calculate the maximum amount to be lent over an agreed period, as well as the security that the property affords.

Small investors might favour the National Savings Bank or National Savings Certificates as their investment outlet.

2.2.2 Stocks and Shares

As an alternative to investment in banks or building societies, an investor may consider stocks and shares, which are normally bought and sold on the Stock Exchange.

In the past, enterprises needing capital for such varied purposes as the formation of business, purchase of land or expansion plans, found that they could not always borrow from their circle of acquaintances. It was also impractical to pay on demand to any lender who wanted his capital returned, because the money had been used for some permanent venture. To raise large amounts of capital, joint stock companies were established; the capital of these companies came from large numbers of investors, who bought shares in the companies. This system is still in existence. If an investor wishes to redeem his capital, he may sell his shares through the Stock Exchange. The Stock Exchange operates as a market place, where buyers and sellers are brought together to sell or buy shares at prices which are determined by the free competition of the open market. Government and local authorities, as well as industrial and commercial concerns, raise capital through the medium of the Stock Exchange.

The Stock Exchange has been in existence since the seventeenth century, and guards its good reputation by enforcing strict conditions and qualifications upon members seeking election. However, on 27 October 1986 changes were made to the organisation and operation of the Stock Exchange (described as 'the Big Bang') The Stock Exchange has needed to be more competitive because of the increasing internationalisation of securities trading. The Big Bang allowed for wider Stock Exchange membership than previously, whereby member firms can be controlled by banks and other financial institutions, giving them access to other sources of capital which enables them to compete on the modern exchange. The Stock Exchange introduced a computerised system SEAQ (Stock Exchange Automated Quotation System) which shows the best prices available for each fully quoted share. The main types of stocks and shares are:

Fixed-interest Securities. An investor will be attracted to these, when he wishes to ensure that his income and capital will be certain. The security quotes a specific return upon the face value. For example, a 5 per cent £1 share will yield a return of 5p each year. The disadvantage of this type of investment is that it may fail to keep pace with inflationary trends; there is no guarantee that income will have the same purchasing power as at present.

Capital required in the public sector may be raised by this type of investment, examples being short-term Local Government loans and Defence Bonds. These types of securities are often referred to as 'Gilts' because they are considered to be 'gilt-edged', an extremely safe form of investment.

Ordinary Shares or Equities. The return on these investments is dependent on the profits a company makes, and may, accordingly, vary from year to year. The possibility of both risk and reward is greater than with the fixed-interest security, so that care needs to be taken in both choice and timing.

In choosing a suitable investment, the likely rate of growth will be important. This may be judged on the past performance of the industry to which the company belongs, and whether or not the company would be responsive and prepared for technological changes.

Preference Shares. These are fixed-dividend shares in joint stock companies, the dividend being paid before ordinary shares. If a company cannot pay at a particular time, its responsibility to do so remains. The interest is cumulative and past arrears of preference interest must be paid before there can be any dividend on the rest of the capital.

Debenture Stocks or Bonds. These are not shares in a business, but loans which create a right to a fixed rate of interest. Holders are entitled to receive their interest before payment of dividends on ordinary shares. Government and public authorities may also borrow money by means of fixed loans which are repayable after a given number of years. These can be bought and sold for their current market value on the Stock Exchange.

2.2.3   Unit Trusts

Unit trusts came into existence in order to reduce the risks to the ordinary investor by giving him the opportunity to spread his investment over a number of companies. There are two independent organisations involved in the formation of a unit trust – a trustee and a management company. The trustee, usually a bank, looks after cash and securities, and ensures that an adequate reserve fund is established, while the management company is responsible for the choice of individual securities. At regular intervals the managers value the securities in the trust and divide the total by the number of units in issue, and in this way values are determined for buying and selling.

2.2.4   Land and Property

Land and property will be considered for investment purposes in Chapter 3.

2.3   YIELD AND DIVIDEND

As stocks and shares are bought and sold, their market value may vary from their original value (nominal value) when issued. A fixed-interest security will have a stated dividend, which may differ from the yield. For example, if a company issued £1 shares yielding a 5 per cent dividend and their market value subsequently increased to £2, then the yield would be 5p on a purchase price of £2, that is, $2^{1}/_{2}$ per cent. Hence

$$\text{Yield} = \frac{\text{nominal value} \times \text{dividend}}{\text{market value}}$$

Comparisons of both yield and security will influence the investor as to his ultimate choice for capital outlay.

3 Land and Property as an Investment

In legal terms, 'land' means the topsoil and all the strata below and the air space above. If a building or roads or paths are constructed upon land, they become part of the land, although it is common practice to refer to 'land and buildings'. The term 'real property' is also used to signify 'land and buildings'.

Real property as a medium for investment differs considerably in its qualities and characteristics compared with the other investment outlets previously mentioned. It is naturally limited in supply and it would be extremely difficult and expensive to create additional land to meet expanding requirements. No two pieces of land are exactly alike in every respect. They will differ in size, topography, locality and condition.

Real property will not be available in regular units for investment as are stocks and shares (there is no equivalent to the £1 share). The size of the investment in the real property market may be such that, generally, it will exclude the small investor unless he wishes to invest in property bonds. To acquire real property the prospective purchaser must usually be considering market values of property units in terms of thousands of pounds, not in tens or hundreds of pounds. Because this type of investment is on a large-scale basis it is regarded favourably by investors such as pension funds and insurance companies, who have large funds available for investment.

3.1 LEGAL ESTATES

A special characteristic of land and buildings is that a piece of land or a building may have legal estates existing in it which are capable of being purchased and sold in the open market. The legal system of land ownership has developed from olden times, but was simplified by the Law of Property Act 1925 which provided two legal estates in land, 'the tenancy in fee simple' and 'the term certain'.

The tenancy in fee simple (or 'the fee simple absolute in possession') is popularly called the freehold. This is the superior interest in land, being perpetual, that is, of an endless period of time. The owner of such an estate has the right to occupy, enjoy and dispose of his property should he so wish, subject to certain limitations to be considered later in this chapter. If he still owns the property on death, it forms part of his estate.

The term certain (or 'the term of years absolute in possession') is popularly called the leasehold. This is created for a specific period of time, such as weekly, monthly, annually or a definite number of years, and gives the leaseholder (or the *lessee* or *tenant*) the right to occupy and enjoy the property over that period of time. He will usually pay rent to the landlord for the benefit of his occupation. Theoretically, at the end of the lease the landlord will be entitled to the property free from the tenant's rights, and he is thus said to own the reversion in the property. In certain cases, however, the tenant may obtain an extension of the period of the lease and continue his occupation. This will occur in the case of certain business tenancies under the Landlord and Tenant Act 1954, and agricultural properties under the Agricultural Holdings Act 1948. Similarly, in certain residential tenancies under Part 1, the Landlord and Tenant Act 1954 and Rent Acts 1965–77, the tenant may have the right to stay in possession. The Housing Act 1980 gives tenants of three or more years tenancy of a public sector dwelling the right to buy at a discounted price. The Housing Act 1985 gives security to certain local authority tenants. Under the Leasehold Reform Act 1967, the tenants of residential properties under ground leases may purchase the freehold at any time during the unexpired period of the lease if they satisfy certain requirements. Under the Leasehold Reform, Housing and Urban Development Act 1993, certain tenants of flats will be able to buy the freehold, subject to conditions.

A tenant may decide that he no longer wishes to occupy the land or property, and he may either 'sublet' or 'assign' the land or property. The lease may require the tenant to obtain the landlord's permission to sublet or assign.

Where the tenant sublets, he grants occupation for a period less than his own, and the new occupant is termed the *sublessee* or *underlessee*; the original lessee under this arrangement may be termed the *sublessor* or *underlessor*. The original lessee (head lessee) will still be responsible to the freeholder for conditions imposed in the lease. Likewise, the sublessee will be responsible to his landlord, the head lessee, for conditions imposed in the sublease; these conditions may be different from those of the head lease.

An assignment differs from a sublease in that the lessee, with his landlord's permission, transfers all his rights to the *assignee* for the full residue of the term. The assignee is thus responsible to the freeholder for satisfying conditions imposed in the original lease.

The lease is an agreement under seal by which a tenancy is granted by a landlord (the lessor) to a tenant (the lessee). If the agreement is executed under hand (written but not under seal), it is termed a *tenancy agreement*, and if created orally it is termed an *oral agreement*. Leases granted for a term of more than three years must be under seal. The lease should state the term of the lease, specify the amount of rent per annum to be paid, when it is to be paid and at what intervals (if any) it will be reviewed. The lease should also state the division of responsibility for repairs and insurance.

In a full repairing and insuring lease the tenant will be responsible for carrying out all repairs and insurance, whereas in an internal repairing lease the tenant will be responsible for internal repairs only, the landlord retaining responsibility for external repairs and insurance.

Where a freeholder grants a lease of building land to a lessee for a long period, such as 99 years, this may be termed a *ground lease*. The rent paid (a ground rent) will be for the use of the land only, and the lessee may erect buildings upon the land for his own occupation or for subletting. At the end of the ground lease, both the land and the buildings upon it will revert to the freeholder, except in certain cases involving residential property, where a lessee may have a right to purchase the freehold interest under the Leasehold Reform Act 1967. (The lessee is given the right to purchase the freehold at any time during the unexpired term of the lease.)

If a lease is granted for the occupation of land and/or buildings, it may be termed an *occupation lease*. If the tenant pays the full rental value of the property this is known as a *rack rent*. (In the case of a full repairing and insuring lease, it may be termed a *net rack rent*.) If, however, the rent paid by the lessee is less than full rental value it is a *head rent* and the lessee enjoys a *profit rent*, that is, the difference between the full rental value (the rack rent) and the rent actually paid (the head rent).

3.1.1 Equitable Interests

There may exist also, in real property, *equitable interests* such as the *tenancy in fee tail* and the *tenancy for life*. These interests are created so that property is settled on a person for life and after his death passes to his eldest son and the heirs of his body. The interest may thus pass from generation to generation unless there are no heirs (in which case the interest reverts to the heirs of the original grantor), or the entail is barred. Under the Settled Land Act 1925, a tenant for life may bar the entail by selling the interest in the settled property, the capital money being paid to the trustees and settled to the same uses as was the land itself.

3.2 CONTROLS ON LAND USAGE

A freeholder or lessee may be restricted from using land or property exactly as he wishes, because he may be subjected to private and/ or statutory controls.

3.2.1 Private Control

Private control on land usage may take the form of restrictive covenants, easements and profits à *prendre*, and licences and wayleaves.

Restrictive covenants are agreements restricting the users of freehold land, which are enforceable not only between the original contracting parties, but also between subsequent successors of those parties. If an owner wishes to sell some of his land, he may continue to live nearby. He may thus impose conditions on the purchaser of the land so as to protect himself as to amenity and privacy, and to maintain the market value of the land he retains. Typical examples of a restrictive covenant would be conditions as to a maximum number and the type of building(s) to be erected on the land and obligations such as fencing or tree-planting requirements. A developer, when selling houses on an estate, may require purchasers to comply with certain obligations, such as the type of fencing to be erected, with a view to maintaining certain minimum standards.

As time passes, it may appear that the restrictive covenant no longer enhances the value of the benefited property, because the surrounding area has altered in character. The covenant may be discharged or modified by agreement of the parties concerned or by application to the Lands Tribunal. The Lands Tribunal may discharge or modify a restrictive covenant if it is considered to be obsolete, or if it prevents the reasonable use of the land for public or private purposes. Or it may be that the discharge or modification would not injure those who benefit from the restriction. If, however, the person who benefits from the restriction would suffer from the discharge or modification, then the landowner will be ordered to pay him compensation.

An easement is a privilege (without the right to take anything from the soil) which the owner of one piece of land, the dominant tenement, has over the other, the servient tenement, to compel its owner to permit something to be done or to refrain from doing something on the servient tenement, for the benefit of the owner of the dominant tenement. Examples are:

(i) Rights of way. A freeholder may have a right to pass over an adjoining owner's land in order to gain access to his own land.

(ii) A freeholder may be prevented from building on his land in a position that will reduce the access of light to the windows of a property on adjoining land.

A profit à *prendre* is a right to take something from another person's land, such as the soil, natural produce of the land or wild animals existing on it, (but a right to take water from a pump or spring is an easement). Easements and profits may be created in the following ways:

(i) Statute. They are frequently created by local Acts of Parliament.

(ii) Express Grant. The express granting of easements and profits may occur between neighbouring owners, such as rights of access and permission to lay a drain over land owned by a neighbour.

(iii) Implied Grant and Long User. When a landowner sells part of his land, certain easements over the land retained are implied in favour of the grantee. Section 62 of the Law of Property Act 1925 deems the items which shall pass with land when it is conveyed, and it may transfer or create such easements as rights of way and rights of light. To avoid this, the vendor may have to incorporate in his conveyance express exclusion of these rights.

If a lawful right has been enjoyed over a long period of time, even though no evidence of its actual grant can be produced, the court will uphold the right assuming it to have a lawful origin. This is termed 'prescription' and may be acquired at common law, by lost modern grant or under the Prescription Act 1832.

At common law, an owner may attempt to show that the usage existed since time immemorial, that is, since 1189 (known as 'prescription at common law'). This is difficult to establish, so that a court may presume that a grant was made subsequent to 1189 but has since been lost (known as 'lost modern grant'). The court may presume a right if 20 years' usage can be shown. The Prescription Act 1832 was passed to overcome difficulties experienced by prescribing at common law or under the doctrine of lost modern grant.

In the case of profits, a claim cannot be defeated on the grounds that the usage commenced after 1189 if 30 years' uninterrupted enjoyment can be proved. If 60 years' uninterrupted enjoyment can be shown, the right becomes absolute unless enjoyed by written consent. The same rule applies to easements, other than those relating to light, except that the respective time periods are 20 and 40 years. Where the access to and use of light by any building has been enjoyed without interruption for 20 years, the right becomes absolute unless it was enjoyed by a consent or agreement in writing.

Easements and profits may be extinguished by statute or release by the dominant tenement. An owner may find that if a way over his land has been used by the public without interruption for a period of 20 years, then it may be deemed to be dedicated as a highway. To prevent this, he must show that he has no intention of dedicating the land as a public highway. This may be achieved by erecting a notice on the land, giving a notice to the appropriate local authority, or closing for one day a year.

Licences and wayleaves are created by statute or with the consent of the landowner. These are rights to enter on another's land for the purposes of erecting, constructing and maintaining works on that land. Annual payments may be made for these rights. Examples are the laying of telephone cables, erection of electric power pylons, traffic signs and advertisements. The written agreement usually provides a period of notice to be given by either party for the extinguishment of the right.

3.3 STATUTORY CONTROLS

3.3.1 Planning Control

Many owners may feel that their land could be used for an alternative purpose, which would make it more valuable, such as residential development on agricultural land. However, they may be restricted by planning control. The present system of planning control originated with the Town and Country Planning Act 1947, which created local planning authorities to prepare plans and control development. Since April 1974, the responsibility for planning may be shared by county and district councils. Under the 1947 Act, local planning authorities were required to prepare development plans for their administrative areas. These plans allocated land for different uses, such as residential, shopping, industrial and roads. They also indicated areas requiring development or redevelopment and designated land subject to acquisition by compulsory purchase.

A new system was introduced by the Town and Country Planning Acts 1968 and 1971, which required local planning authorities to prepare structure and local plans. The local planning authority, after carrying out a survey of its administrative area, prepares a structure plan, which is constantly revised. This plan formulates the local planning authority's policy and general proposals in respect of the development and other use of land in its area. It will include measures for the improvement of the physical environment and management of traffic. The plan should also state the relationship of those proposals to general proposals for the development and other use of land in neighbouring areas, which may be expected to affect that area.

The structure plan is a policy document, and it may not give an individual owner much information about the proposals for his specific piece of land. Such information is more likely to be obtained from a local plan, which may take different forms such as town plans, village plans and action area plans. These plans will establish a planning policy with which individual landowners must comply.

Since 1971, amendments and alterations have been made to the planning system by considerable legislation, the most notable being the Local Government, Planning and Land Act 1980, the Local Government Act 1985, the Town and Country Planning Act 1990 and the Planning and Compensation Act 1991.

In London boroughs and metropolitan districts, current structure and local plans will be replaced by a new kind of development plan known as a *unitary development plan*. Local planning authorities control the development of land by requiring the developer to obtain planning permission. Development is defined in the Town and Country Planning Act 1990 as '(i) the carrying out of building operations, engineering operations, mining operations or other operations in, on, over or under land, or (ii) the making of any material change in the use of any buildings or other land'. To establish whether or not a change of use is material, reference should be made to the Town and Country Planning (Use Classes) Order 1987. For example, changing the use of a cinema to a theatre is not a material change of use, but changing the use of a turf accountant's office to a confectionery shop would be a material change of use.

A prospective developer must make application for planning permission on the appropriate forms to the local planning authority, which has the power to grant unconditionally, grant subject to conditions or refuse planning permission. Where planning permission is granted, it is usually a requirement that the development must be carried out within five years of the permission.

Permission must also be obtained for the provision of new accesses onto highways and display of most advertisements.

Buildings of special architectural of historic interest are protected by the Planning (Listed Buildings and Conservation Areas) Act 1990. Such buildings may be 'listed' by the Secretary of State for National Heritage, copies of these lists being kept by the Secretary of State, the appropriate local planning authorities and other local authorities.

If a local planning authority is of the opinion that an unlisted building of special architectural or historic interest is in danger of demolition or alteration which would adversely affect its character, it may apply to the Secretary of State to list the building. In the meantime, a building preservation notice would be served on the owner and occupier. Permission must be obtained to demolish, extend or alter listed buildings. Persons carrying out unauthorised works will be liable to imprisonment and/or a fine.

Areas of special architectural or historic interest may be designated as 'conservation areas'.

A local planning authority may also make tree preservation orders as directed by the Town and Country Planning Act 1990. These may apply to individual trees, groups of trees or woodland areas. Such trees may not be felled, lopped or topped without permission.

3.3.2 Building and Other Controls

Local authorities have control over the construction of buildings by powers derived from the Building Regulations 1991 and subsequent amendments. Approval must be obtained before construction of buildings can take place. Application forms and plans must be submitted to the local authority. The regulations prescribe the standards of construction and materials to be used. Officers of the local authority have power to inspect building works as they proceed, at specified stages, and to enforce the provisions of the Regulations.

Local authorities must implement the provisions of the Offices,

Shops and Railway Premises Act 1963 which are concerned with cleanliness, overcrowding, temperature, ventilation and lighting of offices, shops and railway premises; also for the provision of suitable and sufficient sanitary conveniences and washing facilities, the provision of drinking water, the safety of the premises and machinery, first-aid facilities and for provision of means of escape in case of fire. This legislation may require an owner of one of these classes of buildings to undertake considerable expenditure to put the property in order.

In the case of factories, similar provisions are contained in the Factories Act 1961, the enforcing authority being the local authority, or, if the building has mechanical power, the factory inspector.

The Fire Precautions Act 1971 requires that certain premises designated by the Secretary of State for Home Affairs shall have a certificate issued by the fire authority, which states that the means of escape and provision for fire fighting and warning of fire are adequate. These premises include hotels, boarding houses, places of entertainment, institutions providing treatment or care and those used for purposes of teaching, training or research.

With regard to housing, local authorities have the power to implement the provisions of the Housing Acts 1957–84 (now consolidated in the Housing Act 1985) and subsequent legislation. They have the right to order owners of insanitary houses to repair them at reasonable expense or demolish them. They may also declare areas to be *clearance* areas, where houses (singly or in groups) need to be demolished and the sites redeveloped. *General improvement areas* may be established under the Housing Act 1969, and in these cases the local authority may require a landlord to provide standard amenities (bath, wash basin, water closet, sink and hot and cold water supply) in his properties. The landlord receives financial assistance through local authority payment of improvement grants.

The Defective Premises Act 1972 places a duty of care on all persons concerned with the provision of new dwellings, including conversion and enlargement of existing buildings. The work is to be done in a workmanlike or professional manner with proper materials so that the dwelling is fit for habitation. It does not apply to Scotland or Northern Ireland, nor in those cases where the Secretary of State has approved a scheme which gives equal or better protection to the purchaser, such as the National House-building Council scheme.

The Caravan Sites and Control of Development Act 1960 provides that, subject to certain exemptions specified in the First Schedule of the Act, no occupier of land may allow any part of his land to be used as a caravan site for residential or holiday purposes unless he obtains a site licence. Local authorities have a duty under the Caravan Sites Act 1968 to provide sites for gipsies, and are also given powers to control unauthorised gipsy encampments when there is adequate provision of authorised sites.

3.4 CHARACTERISTICS OF LAND AND PROPERTY

The investor in land and property, as with any other source of investment, requires an annual return on his capital; this is obtained by purchasing an interest in real property and obtaining an annual return in the form of rent.

A purchaser of an interest in real property may buy for personal occupation, and he may be in competition with an investor. In his choice of property, a purchaser for personal occupation will pay special attention to the available social and commercial facilities. In the case of housing, these will include proximity to schools, shops, entertainment and employment. The investor will be concerned with yield and will compare with the ideal investment.

A prospective occupier of real property may have the choice between purchasing the freehold interest or leasing. He should consider the advantages, such as security, which purchasing would normally give him. The capital to purchase the premises may be obtained by mortgage borrowing. The occupier should compare the interest repayments on his mortgage with the rent that he would be expected to pay. He will only be prepared to pay more in interest repayments than rent if the advantages of being a freeholder compared with a lessee make it worthwhile.

There are certain characteristics relating to real property that will affect the security of both capital and income.

3.4.1 External Influences

Land and buildings vary in their condition with consequent effect on value. Variations may arise from natural consequences, such as the nature of the soil and adverse weather conditions, creating such problems as flooding, subsidence and damage due to lightning. Damage may also occur to land and buildings due to human activities such as vandalism, accidental damage, fire and hostilities.

Insurance cover can provide a safeguard against the financial loss arising from physical risks, and this may be the responsibility of the landlord or the tenant, according to the terms of the lease. The landlord often insures the premises and recovers the premium from the tenant; the occupant may insure the contents of the premises.

3.4.2 Deterioration of the Structure

The physical life of a building is often difficult to estimate. Building techniques and materials are constantly changing, and it is likely that buildings in the future will not be planned to last as long as they have in the past. However, in order to ensure a reasonable standard for occupation, it will be necessary for sums of money to be expended on repairs and decoration throughout the life of the building.

Standards are constantly changing, so to ensure a reasonable level of rent the property has to be improved and renovated. For example, the occupiers of multi-storey office buildings may expect the latest types of central heating, air conditioning and lift systems. The occupiers of houses may in the future expect a security system to be a standard item.

If the investor is responsible for maintenance of property under the terms of a lease, he may provide for these costs by setting aside an annual sum out of the rent he receives.

The age of a building will also be reflected in the yield that an investor will expect; thus an old building, likely to be demolished in the foreseeable future, will show a higher yield than one with a reasonable life, although the site might have development potential value in excess of the value of the obsolescent building.

3.4.3 Changes in Taste and Demand

The rental value of a building may be reduced because the purpose of the building no longer satisfies a demand. An investor must attempt to anticipate whether or not a building will continue to be functional in its present form, and this will affect the yield he may expect from the investment.

Examples of changes in the use of buildings in recent years are the decline of the local cinema in favour of the bingo hall, the need for public houses to provide more comfortable accommodation and entertainment, in shopping the trends towards the larger self-service unit and the increased popularity of food takeaways and video film hire shops.

3.4.4 Effect of Adjacent Activities

The value of property may be affected by both existing and proposed developments within the area. A prospective investor should inspect the development plans operative in his area and consult with the local planning authority so as to be aware of any developments that may affect the value of the particular property.

Examples. (1) The provision of motorways or trunk roads, airports and new railway stations will affect the value of all types of property units in that area.
(2) The building of an industrial estate may be detrimental to neighbouring residential property.
(3) The provision of a new shopping unit may alter the values of other shops in the vicinity.
(4) The building of a new further educational establishment may affect property values in the area, because demand will be created for rented residential accommodation. There may also be an influx of vehicles into the area.
(5) The building of crematoria, sewage-treatment works and electricity substations may all reduce the value of surrounding property.

3.4.5 Economic Activities

The demand for land is affected by economic activities and national, regional and local policies.

Policies of expanding old towns, improving and altering communications and decentralising offices and industries to less buoyant areas will affect the land values in the areas concerned.

There may be some areas that are particularly dependent for their livelihood on a specific economic activity such as coal-mining. If that activity becomes uneconomic and ceases, then it will have serious effects upon all types of property in that area. In this situation public authorities, both central and local, will encourage other industries to establish themselves in the area to maintain a balanced economy.

3.4.6 Changes in Legislation

An investor may not easily anticipate changes in legislation that will affect property values. Land and property are constantly affected by new legislation, which may later be repealed when there is a change of government.

3.4.7 Inflation

Inflationary trends will be a problem with any type of investment. In the case of fixed-interest securities, the reduction in the real value may have substantially exceeded the aggregate interest earned over the same period. The problem will be apparent in the case of property, where the investor's return (the rent) is a fixed amount to be received over a long period of time. In this situation, the yield must be high enough to allow for both the depreciation in purchasing power of the fixed amount of rent and a fair return on capital.

To protect himself against the effects of inflation a landlord should make provision for regular reviews of rent when granting a lease. In the past, many ground leases were created with a fixed rent and these were considered to be secure investments. Nowadays these would probably be granted subject to three-year reviews, and this would also be a realistic review period for commercial and residential letting.

The rent to be paid at the review periods may be established in various ways as described below.

(i) The rent may be predetermined at the commencement of the lease. In this case, the landlord must attempt to anticipate the future pattern of inflation as a percentage increase per annum and adjust the current rental value accordingly. This requires expert knowledge of economic trends, and often a landlord will find that he has underestimated the inflationary increase.

(ii) A better alternative may be to state in the lease when rent is to be reviewed and agreed between the parties. A provision could be included that if the parties fail to agree, the matter will be referred to a qualified valuer. The lease may state that the rent should be reviewed to market value with a stipulation that the rent would not be lower than the existing rent under the lease.

However, during the last few years, because of recessionary trends, rents in some situations may have shown a 'down-turn'. A tenant may not accept the incorporation of 'upwards-only' rent review clauses into leases.

(iii) In commercial property, the rent to be reviewed may be expressed as an agreed percentage on the annual turnover of the business.

(iv) Where new buildings are constructed for investment purposes, the rental values will be influenced by the increase in building costs. An investor will obviously expect a fair return upon his capital cost in the form of rent. If rents do not keep in step with building costs, then the rate of construction of investment properties is likely to slow down. This would create a greater demand by tenants for existing premises and the rents of these would increase accordingly.

3.4.8 Relationship to Other Investment Sources

Land as an investment is in competition with other sources of investment. If yields generally are in an upward direction, then property investments must follow the same pattern, otherwise money will be withdrawn from property and invested elsewhere. Because of the size and nature of the investment, property is usually a long-term investment, which will not be too severely affected by day-to-day market activities unless these persist. However, the availability of credit and borrowing facilities will affect demand for property purchase.

3.4.9 Costs of Transactions

Negotiations involving purchases and sales of land usually take considerable time to complete and involve heavy legal costs compared with other sources of investment.

3.5   DETERMINATION OF RENTAL VALUE

The rental value of a commercial property is the amount that a prospective tenant can afford to pay for its occupation. The tenant occupies the property for the purpose of making profit, so that the value of occupation to him will be dependent on what he can earn there. There may be instances where a property has a special value for a particular tenant; for example, the property is adjacent to premises which he already occupies and/or owns.

In the case of residential property, occupation is a need and does not usually serve a profit-making function. In many cases, the rent will be established by statutory rent control, which will determine the maximum amount of rent that may be charged at a particular time.

If rent is dependent on profit, it will be affected by the economic state of the country and many of the characteristics of land and property as previously considered. The rack rental value of property may be calculated at a particular time in several ways:

(i) By reference to the rent currently being paid. This may be a reasonable guide but it could be less than the rack rental value. It may have been fixed at a date in the past, and rental values have since increased due to inflationary trends.

The rent paid may, at the commencement of the lease, be less than the full rental value at that time. This may occur because there is a special relationship between the landlord and tenant such as father and son or the lessor is a parent company of the lessee. Another reason may be that the tenant agrees to pay a capital sum, termed a premium, for the benefit of paying less rent than the rack rental value.

(ii) By comparison with similar property. If properties are owner-occupied, vacant or held on long-established leases, then, to determine their current rental values, it may be necessary to compare them with the general levels of similar properties in the same district. The practical difficulty of this method is that no two properties are exactly the same, so that the value of the comparable property may have to be adjusted to take into account differences in age, location, condition and other matters.

The units of comparison will vary according to the type of land and property; for example, agricultural and building land may be compared per hectare (or acre) and residential, industrial and commercial property per square metre (or square foot) of floor area.

(iii) By considering rent as a proportion of turnover or profit. This method of calculating rack rental value is based on the requirements of the tenant. A prospective tenant of a commercial property will calculate his likely turnover, costs, an allowance for interest on capital employed in the business, salary and rates. The balance will represent profit and he will then determine the proportion of this to be allocated to rent. Hence prospective tenants may differ in the way that they calculate the rent that they are prepared to pay with resultant variations in the figures obtained.

Example. Shop premises are available for letting. A, who occupies other premises, wishes to expand his business and estimates that he could earn a profit of £30 000 per annum in the shop to be leased. He is prepared to pay 30 per cent of his profit in rent, that is, 30 per cent of £30 000 which is £9000 per annum.

B, entering into business for the first time, estimates that he could earn a profit of £20 000 per annum in this shop. Because he is anxious to commence his own business, he is prepared to pay 50 per cent of his profit in rent, that is, 50 per cent of £20 000 which is £10 000 per annum.

The landlord would negotiate with *B*, but may not readily accept £10 000 per annum, because this would not provide the yield he anticipates from his investment. He has recently purchased the freehold interest in the shop for £150 000. He expects a 7 per cent return, which is £10 500 per annum.

The rent eventually paid would be dependent upon the level of demand for the occupancy of the shop.

(iv) By relating the rent to cost. Where land has buildings erected upon it, the rent will consist of two elements. There will be an annual return for the use of the land itself, which will be dependent upon supply and demand. There will also be an annual repayment for the cost of the building, which should be an appropriate yield on the capital outlay.

Example. *A* has recently purchased a building plot for £60 000. He has built a house on the land, which has cost £60 000. Calculate the rack rental value per annum.

The rack rental value comprises

(i) Return on the value of the land

   A requires 8 per cent on £60 000 = £4800

(ii) Return on capital outlay of building

   A requires 10 per cent on £60 000 = £6000

   Rack rental value per annum = £10 800

This method may be criticised because rent is calculated according to the landlord's expectations and not necessarily what those in the market would be prepared to pay.

3.6 RENT AND CAPITAL VALUE

Capital or market value may be defined as the amount of money which may be obtained for an interest at a particular time from those individuals who are able and willing to purchase it.

It has already been established that those able and willing to purchase land and property for investment require a return in the form of rent per annum. However, the investor may incur outgoings, which are annual expenses such as management costs and repairs. These must be deducted from the rent to give the amount which constitutes the true return – the net income per annum. Hence

net income per annum = rent received per annum –
outgoings per annum

If an investor expects a return of 8 per cent per annum from a prospective purchase of property and the net income per annum is £10 000, then he will be prepared to purchase at a capital sum of which £10 000 is 8 per cent, that is

$$£10\ 000 \times \frac{100}{8} = £125\ 000$$

Hence

net income per annum $\times \dfrac{100}{\text{rate of interest}}$ = capital value

This is termed capitalising the net income and the multiplier is termed years' purchase (YP), so that

net income per annum $\times$ years' purchase = capital value

3.7 OUTGOINGS

The responsibility for the payment of outgoings should be a condition contained in the lease or tenancy agreement.

Leases for a long period (21 years and over) are often full repairing and insuring, that is, the tenant will be responsible for all repairs and insurance. In the case of weekly and monthly tenancies, the landlord is usually responsible for the payment of all outgoings.

The calculation of an annual allowance for landlord's outgoings is necessary in order to arrive at net income per annum. The practical difficulty of calculating outgoings is that they will vary from year to year, due to such matters as increases in repair costs and changes in general and water rates. The amount of liability for outgoings that a landlord incurs under the terms of the lease will affect the security of his interest, so influencing his yield and the years' purchase. The outgoings most commonly taken into account are as follows.

3.7.1   Rent Payable to a Superior Landlord

With a leasehold interest, a lessee may relet the premises to a sub-lessee. He must deduct from the rent he receives any rent which is payable by him to the freeholder or lessor. This may be a ground rent or an occupation rent.

3.7.2   Repairs

Repairs may be the most difficult of outgoings to assess, and consideration must be given to the age and condition of the property and the terms of the lease. If repairs are the responsibility of the landlord, various methods of estimation are available.

(i) By reference to past costs. If records have been kept for repair costs expended on a particular property over a number of years, these may be used as a basis for estimating an annual allowance. For example, assuming records show annual repair costs over the last five years of £2300, £1900, £2500, £2650 and £2900, then the average cost per annum is £2450 (12250/5). If this is used as an annual allowance, it may be misleading if there is a major item of renovation or rebuilding required in the near future. This item will not be reflected in the previous five years' costs. Taking an average of previous costs will not allow for future increases in costs.

(ii) By a planned maintenance programme. An inspection of the property is carried out and a schedule of dilapidation and repair items prepared. An estimate is made of the periods at which items will need to be carried out and their estimated cost. This is then expressed on an annual basis.

(iii) By expressing repairs as a percentage of rack rental value. The two methods previously described of ascertaining a repair allowance are dependent upon having a detailed knowledge of the property. If this is not available, the annual allowance may be expressed as a percentage of net rack rental value. This will vary according to the type of property, but the following figures provide a general guide for use in later calculations.

	External repairs (per cent)	Internal repairs (per cent)
Offices, factories and warehouses	10	5
Shops	5	5
Residential property	30 to 40	10 to 20

In the case of residential property, repairs are a very variable item; indeed local authorities and statutory undertakings may expend most of the rent received from residential property on repairs.

(iv) By the landlord determining what he can afford. A landlord may decide, when he invests in land and property, the maximum amount per annum he can expend on repairs. This is not a good method, because, if a landlord has a pre-fixed allowance, this may not always be sufficient. The Defective Premises Act 1972 states that, where premises are let under a tenancy which puts on the landlord an obligation to the tenant for the maintenance or repair of the premises, the landlord owes to all persons who might reasonably expect to be affected by defects in the state of the premises, a duty to take such care as is reasonable in all the circumstances to see that they are reasonably safe from personal injury or from damage to their property caused by a relevant defect. This duty is owed by the landlord if he knows of the relevant defect either by being notified by the tenant or if he ought in all the circumstances to have known. It is of extreme importance that a landlord inspects his premises regularly and keeps them well maintained.

3.7.3 Insurances

The lease will establish who is responsible for the obtaining of insurance cover in the first instance and who is responsible for the maintaining of adequate cover thereafter. In relation to injuries to third parties, the landlord should have a Property Owner's Liability Policy. He should ensure that this covers his liabilities under the Defective Premises Act 1972.

A lease may be specific, setting out the exact risks to be dealt with such as fire, flood and damage due to vandalism. In assessing an annual premium, this will be wholly dependent on the sum insured. The sum insured, based on reinstatement cost, must be assessed competently, taking into account the standard of construction of the actual building. The reinstatement cost should be prepared as a cost estimate by a quantity surveyor. The sum insured should be reviewed at regular intervals to take account of increased building costs. The landlord should also ensure that his policy has adequate provision for loss of rent during a rebuilding period. Special insurance is available for such items as lifts and boilers. The deduction from rent for insurance will be the annual premium paid by the landlord. If this is not known, a percentage of net rack rental value may be taken, a reasonable allowance being $2\frac{1}{2}$ to 5 per cent.

3.7.4   Management

A landlord will need to inspect his property and ensure that his tenant is complying with the obligations contained in the lease. He will also have to collect the rent due to him.

In the case of full repairing and insuring leases, the cost of management may be regarded as a factor affecting security and be reflected in the yield. In weekly and monthly tenancies, however, management may be a costly item because rent is probably collected fortnightly. The amounts may be modest but the time and trouble taken is comparatively extravagant. In these cases, 10 per cent of the net rack rental value may be deducted as an annual outgoing. In properties where services such as porters and lifts are provided, 5 per cent of net rack rental value may be deducted. If management is undertaken by professional experts appointed by the landlord, their scale of fees may give an indication of the amount to be allowed for management.

3.7.5   Landlord's Services

Where a building is let in multiple occupation, it may be convenient for the landlord to provide certain services himself. This is

common practice in flats and offices, where the landlord may repair and redecorate common parts, provide central heating, lighting to common parts, carpeting, lifts and porters. The landlord may
recover his costs by including an amount in the rent. In this case
services should be deducted from rent as an outgoing, in order to
arrive at net income. Alternatively the landlord may serve an account for services probably at half-yearly intervals.

The landlord must decide whether the cost of services is to be
borne equally by his tenants or apportioned according to the respective floor areas occupied by each tenant or by some other
method. It is essential that the landlord attempts to take account
of rising costs in the arrangements he makes with his tenants.

3.7.6 Bad Debts and Voids

A landlord may anticipate that there is a risk because his tenant
may default with his rent. There may also be instances where the
type of property attracts tenants who are likely to occupy the premises
for short periods and then terminate their tenancy. The property
may not be relet immediately, so that there may be *voids* in the
receipt of rent. It is not usual to deduct an allowance for bad debts
or voids as an outgoing. These are factors that seriously affect
security of income and should be reflected in the yield.

3.7.7 Rent charges

A rent charge occurred when an owner of an interest in land sold
that interest at a value less than full market value. In lieu of the
reduction in purchase price, he imposed upon the purchaser an
annual charge, which may be perpetual or might have been for a
fixed period of time. This charge will be enforceable upon subsequent owners of that land.

For example, a freeholder sold land worth a capital value of
£9000 subject to a rent charge in perpetuity. If he required
the rent charge to give a 10 per cent return on the capital he
has forfeited, then it would be £100 per annum, which is 10
per cent of £1000.

Rent charges have never been popular, and the Rent Charge
Act 1977 prohibited the creation of new ones (subject to excep-
tions), and provided that existing rent charges should terminate
after a further 60 years.

3.7.8   Property Taxes and Charges

(a) Commercial Property

General rates and water and sewerage charges are usually an occupier's payment; in certain cases a landlord may pay them to the local authority and then recoup them from the tenant. If a rent includes rates it is termed an 'inclusive' rent and rates must be deducted as an outgoing. If the occupant pays his own rates direct to the local authority, the rent is termed an 'exclusive' rent.

The Valuation Officer of the Board of Inland Revenue has the authority to prepare a valuation list for those properties which are subjected to rating. Each rateable hereditament has a *rateable value* which is assessed taking into account age, size, condition, location and facilities of the property. The rateable value is multiplied to a Uniform Business Rate (UBR), which gives the annual liability for general rates.

(b) Residential Property

Residential properties are subject to Council Tax. Each dwelling is allocated to one of eight bands according to its open market capital value on 1 April 1991, and the tax is calculated according to the allocated band. Water and sewerage charges are based on the 1989/90 Rateable Value.

Water and sewerage charges are usually an occupier's liability.

3.8   CHARACTERISTICS OF DIFFERENT TYPES OF, AND INTERESTS IN, PROPERTY

3.8.1 Ground Rents

Where ground is let by a freeholder to a lessee (or by a lessee to a sublessee) for building operations, it is usually let at a ground rent, which is for the use of the land. Where buildings have been erected upon the land the ground rent is secured because the rent received by the landlord is a small proportion of the full rack rental value of the land and buildings. For example, if a ground rent is £100 per annum and the net rack rental value per annum of the land and buildings is £5000, then the ground rent is 50 times secured.

In the past, ground leases have been let for periods varying from 99 to 999 years at a ground rent fixed for the entire period. This situation nowadays is unattractive in terms of investment because the rent being fixed does not provide a hedge against inflation, and an investor will probably expect a return in excess of 10 per cent.

With recent ground leases landlords have often required periodic rent reviews, the amount of rent to be paid at each review probably being a percentage of the rack rental value of the land and buildings. The rent to be paid during the building period may be a *peppercorn rent*, a minimal amount. The yield expected by an investor will depend upon the length of the lease, the periods for rent reviews and the type of building.

3.8.2 Agricultural Land

Agricultural land is regarded as a secure type of investment and in recent years has proved to be attractive to institutional investors. Rental values will be dependent on

(i) The general situation of the land, which affects the market for produce and the availability of labour.

(ii) The topography of the land and climate of the district.

(iii) The size of the holding. Generally, smaller farms will yield a higher rent per hectare (acre) than a larger one.

(iv) Natural features such as type and condition of the soil, level of the water table and type and condition of hedges.

(v) The condition of fences and approach roads and the efficiency of land drainage.

(vi) Availability of services such as water supply to both farm buildings and troughs, main drainage and electricity.

(vii) The provision and condition of dwellings and farm buildings.

Buildings must be of suitable construction for the housing of livestock and machinery and the storage of crops and fertilisers. Dwellings for employees are a desirable requirement since they may be the means of attracting labour; they should, however, at least have the standard amenities.

The rents of agricultural holdings may be reviewed every three years, and tenants are usually responsible for repairs and maintenance of land and buildings. The landlord may retain responsibility for the structural parts of the farmhouse; if the lease does not mention repair responsibilities then the provisions of the Agriculture (Maintenance, Repair and Insurance of Fixed Equipment) Regulations 1973 will apply.

Successive governments have attempted to ensure that the agricultural industry is encouraged by subsidies and grants to increase production and carry out improvements. The industry is being re-organised as part of the agricultural policy of the European Union. The production methods of the industry have been streamlined during recent years with improved machinery and the grouping of small holdings into larger businesses operated by companies.

3.8.3   Residential Properties

Flats. The majority of flats are built for sale and not for renting. When flats are built for renting, they are mainly provided by local authorities and often incorporated in a development with other types of property.

The private investor may find that the building of flats is prohibitive, because of the high and increasing cost of construction. Some flats, however, are provided by Housing Associations, which are voluntary, independent and non-profit-making bodies. Where flats are available for rent, they are usually considered to be a good investment. The rental value will be dependent upon the condition and locality of the premises, the availability of services, lifts and boilers, and the provision of services such as porterage and cleaning.

However, there may be far-reaching effects on rented flats with the implementation of the Leasehold Reform, Housing and Urban Development Act 1993 (see earlier).

Dwelling houses. Over 50 per cent of the housing stock in the United Kingdom is owner-occupied. New houses built in the private sector are seldom made available for renting because there is little incentive for private developers to build and lease. Hence local authorities are given wide powers to acquire land and provide schemes of rented accommodation.

Dwelling houses that are let are subjected to considerable legislation relating to security of tenure and rent control. In many instances, landlords are restricted as to the amount of rent they can charge to their property. The carrying out of repairs and the provision of insurance cover is often the responsibility of the landlord, and in many cases this may prove to be a costly outgoing.

The yield expected by an investor will obviously vary considerably, being dependent upon the age, locality and condition of the property, the age and type of tenant and whether or not the property is subject to rent control.

3.8.4 Shops

The pattern of shopping has varied considerably over the last twenty years, and the many categories of shops can be classified as

Hypermarkets. These are large-scale developments trading as single concerns on a self-service basis with good communications and car parking for at least 1000 cars. They usually provide a considerable range of competitively priced products because of the substantial turnover.

Regional shopping centres. These are located on out-of-town sites and rely on attracting the car-borne shopper. They incorporate branches of national department stores and provide a wider range of shops and a greater selection of luxury goods than hypermarkets. They may also provide community facilities.

Central area shops. Shops on prime sites in towns and cities and those incorporated in new urban developments are very much in demand by prospective tenants and this is reflected in their rental value. Because of the location secure tenants, such as established multiple-store companies, will often compete for the occupation of these sites. The amount of trading may be influenced considerably by the amount of car parking facilities for shoppers.

Suburban shops. Despite the existence of large urban shopping centres, there will still be a demand by local residents for shops on the outskirts of towns and cities. These shops will provide services to their customers that are required at less than weekly intervals, such as provision of food, newspapers and postal services.

Local shops. This type of shop, probably occupied by a sole trader, is usually located within a residential area and provides a convenience service. The success of local shops has in the past largely stemmed from the varied range of goods they provide, the extensive hours of opening and personal service.

Location is obviously important in determining the rental value of shop premises, but there are also other factors:

(i) The area of frontage and its layout for the display of goods. A prospective tenant will need to decide whether or not he should renew the shop front.

(ii) The condition of the property and its sanitary arrangements. The property must comply with the requirements of the Offices, Shops and Railways Premises Act 1963.

(iii) The layout of the interior and standard of lighting.

(iv) Access at the rear for delivery. This is an advantage, where there are parking restrictions at the front of the property.

(v) Any upper floors within the premises. These may be used as part of the shop or they could be let separately as offices or residential accommodation.

From an investment viewpoint, the type of business of an existing tenant may affect the yield. Certain businesses such as those dealing in essential foodstuffs and other necessities are generally secure. There may be more risks for businesses dealing in luxury items, such as electrical goods.

3.8.5   Offices

The types of premises used as offices may be converted dwelling-houses, part of a mixed development or purpose-built office accommodation. In areas where restrictions on the provision of new accommodation are imposed, demand will increase for existing office space and rentals will increase. Evidence of this can be found in the central area of London, where rents are probably five or six times higher than for similar premises in provincial cities.

The following factors are relevant when assessing rental value and considering the accommodation as an investment medium.

(i) The premises must comply with the Offices, Shops and Railway Premises Act 1963.

(ii) The location of the office may be an influence on the obtaining of suitable staff. For example women may be more attracted to working in a central area than out-of-town.

(iii) If the building is let to a number of tenants, it may command more rent than if let to a single tenant. However, the extent of management by the landlord may increase, where there are more tenants in the building. Generally, landlords prefer to let to a single tenant of good standing.

(iv) The terms of leases may differ considerably. If offices in a building are let to several tenants, the landlord may retain responsibility for repair of the structure and common parts of the building.

(v) The landlord may provide certain services such as lighting, heating, carpeting, porterage and lifts. The cost may be recovered as part of the rent or as a separate service charge collected each six months or annually.

(vi) In high-rise buildings rents may vary from one floor to another. For example, the lower floors may be considered to have more prestige value than upper floors, although this will depend upon the quality of the building and efficiency of lift services.

There is every indication that demand for office accommodation will continue, particularly for small units in central areas.

3.8.6 Industrial Premises

The demand for factories and warehouses is dependent upon the economic state of industry and the capacity of firms to expand, and the provision of new industrial accommodation.

Recently, there has been an upsurge of demand for rented industrial accommodation particularly for purpose-built units. There is, however, a large number of obsolete premises which need to be demolished and rebuilt.

Location in relation to transport systems, availability of labour and markets is an important factor, but the following should also be considered.

(i) The construction, condition and facilities of the buildings. The premises must comply with the requirements of Factories Acts with regard to such items as means of escape in case of fire, heating, ventilation, natural light and sanitary accommodation.

(ii) The general layout of the buildings. The buildings should have good facilities for delivery and despatch of goods, storage and handling. The height of the buildings may be important for certain manufacturing processes. It will be an advantage if the buildings can be readily adapted for other uses.

(iii) The provision of facilities for employees such as car parking, canteens and social areas (for example, bars and games rooms).

3.8.7 Other Types of Property

The valuation of more specialised types of property such as cinemas, theatres and hotels and interests connected with minerals and sporting rights are considered to be beyond the scope of this book.

3.9   PATTERNS OF YIELDS

Table 3.1 indicates suggested yields which investors may expect from different types of property. It must be emphasised that this table gives a general guide only, and yields will frequently be fluctuating depending upon the investment market.

Table 3.1   Suggested Yields for Property Investments (yields for freehold interests let on a rack rent basis)

Description of Property	Yield (per cent)	Remarks
Offices:		Varies according to design, amount of lettable space and general economic activity.
Central London	7–8	
Greater London	9–10	
South East	8–9	
Regions	8–9	
Shops:		Dependent on position, type of unit and type of tenant (e.g. multiple, small trader). Prime retail property in cathedral towns and regional centres has retained its scarcity value so that yields have been relatively stable.
Cathedral Towns	5–6	
Regional Centres	5–6	
Subregional Centres	6–7	
Market Towns	7–8	
Retail Warehouses	8–9	
Industrials:		Economic recovery has not yet affected large scale take-up of vacant industrial space. Depends on adaptability, location, proximity to transport systems, availability of labour.
Greater London and South East	8–9	
Regions	8–9	
Agricultural land:		Number of transactions subject to tenancy decreasing. Market is static. Affected by European Community agricultural policies.
Arable Units	5–8	
Dairy	4–7	
Mixed and Hill Farms	6–8	

4 The Mathematics of Valuation

The purpose of this chapter is to study the mathematics needed as a preliminary requisite to the solving of valuation problems in subsequent chapters.

The following abbreviations are extensively used

i = rate of interest per annum expressed as a decimal (rate of interest/100)

n = term of years (or the number of terms in a series)

4.1 ARITHMETICAL PROGRESSIONS

An arithmetical progression is a series of numbers, in which each term is formed from the preceding one by adding the same number to it. The amount to be added each time is termed the *common difference* and it may have a positive or a negative value.

The formula for calculating the sum of an arithmetical progression may be derived as follows.

Assume that an arithmetical progression has n terms, and that the first term is a and the common difference is d. The sequence of numbers emerges by adding d to the preceding number, and the series develops thus a, $a + d$, $a + 2d$, $a + 3d$ ... up to and including $a + (n - 1)d$ this being the last term. (The characteristic of d is one less than its place in the series, so that for the nth term, d has a characteristic of $n - 1$.)

It can be seen that the average of the first and last terms is the same as the average of the second and the next-to-last terms so that the average for the whole series is the average of the first and last terms, namely

43

$$\frac{a + (a + (n - 1)d)}{2}$$

The sum of the arithmetical progression Sn is thus

$$Sn = \frac{n}{2}(a + a + (n - 1)d)$$

$$= \frac{n}{2}(2a + (n - 1)d)$$

Example. A man purchased a property last year, and during his first year of ownership has spent £150 on repairs. He anticipates that this amount will increase by £50 each year. What will be his total expenditure on repairs at the end of 14 years?

$$Sn = \frac{n}{2}(2a + (a - 1)d)$$

where Sn = the total expenditure, n = 14, a = 150 and d = 50. Substituting in the formula

$$\text{Total expenditure} = \frac{14}{2}[(2 \times 150) + (13 \times 50)]$$

$$= 7 \times (300 + 650)$$

$$= 7 \times 950$$

$$= £6650$$

Example. Three consecutive numbers in an arithmetical progression have a total sum of 75 and a product of 15 000. Find the numbers.

Let the numbers be represented by $a - d$, a, $a + d$. Then

$$(a - d) + a + (a + d) = 75$$

$$3a = 75$$

$$a \text{ (the second term)} = 25$$

But

$$a(a - d)(a + d) = 15\,000$$

$$a(a^2 - d^2) = 15\,000$$

$$25\,(25^2 - d^2) = 15\,000$$

$$15\,625 - 25d^2 = 15\,000$$

$$d^2 = \frac{15\,625 - 15\,000}{25}$$

$$= \frac{625}{25} = 25$$

$$d = \pm\,5$$

The three numbers are, therefore, 20, 25, and 30.

Example. The sum of the first nine terms of an arithmetical progression is 37.8 and the common difference is 0.2. Find the first term of the series.

$$Sn = \frac{n}{2}\,[2a + (n - 1)d]$$

where $Sn = 37.8$, $n = 9$ and $d = 0.2$. Therefore

$$37.8 = \frac{9}{2}\,[2a + (8 \times 0.2)]$$

$$37.8 = 4.5\,(2a + 1.6)$$

$$37.8 = 9a + 7.2$$

$$9a = 30.6$$

$$a = \frac{30.6}{9}$$

$$= 3.4$$

4.2 GEOMETRICAL PROGRESSIONS

A geometrical progression is a series of numbers in which each term is formed from the preceding one by multiplying it by a constant factor, this factor being termed the *common ratio*.

The formula for calculating the sum of a geometrical progression may be derived as follows.

Assume that a geometrical progression has n terms, the first term is a and the common ratio is r. The standard form of a geometrical progression is

$a,\ ar,\ ar^2,\ ar^3 \ldots$ up to and including ar^{n-1}

Let Sn = the sum of n terms

$Sn = a + ar + ar^2 + ar^3 \ldots$ up to and including $ar^{n-2} + ar^{n-1}$ (1)

Multiplying each term by r, gives

$r\,Sn = ar + ar^2 + ar^3 + ar^4 \ldots$ up to and including $ar^{n-1} + ar^n$ (2)

Subtracting equation 1 from equation 2 gives

$$r\,Sn - Sn = ar^n - a$$

$$Sn(r - 1) = a(r^n - 1)$$

$$Sn = \frac{a(r^n - 1)}{r - 1}$$

If r has a negative value or is a fraction less than unity, the formula is reversed thus

$$Sn = \frac{a(1 - r^n)}{1 - r}$$

Example. A property owner estimates that his repair costs will increase by 11 per cent each year. What will be the total cost of repairs at the end of 12 years, if his first year costs are £120?

In the geometrical progression formula

$$Sn = \frac{a(r^n - 1)}{r - 1}$$

Sn = total expenditure, $a = 120$

$r = 1.11$ and $n = 12$

Thus total expenditure $= \dfrac{120(1.11^{12} - 1)}{1.11 - 1}$

$$= \dfrac{120(3.496 - 1)}{0.11}$$

$$= £2723$$

Example. Find the ninth term of the series $+ 2, - 4, + 8, - 16, \ldots$ In this series $a = 2$ and $r = - 2$. Hence the ninth term is

$$ar^{9-1} = 2 \times (- 2)^8$$

$$= 2 \times 256$$

$$= + 512$$

4.3 SIMPLE INTEREST

If money is loaned or invested the owner of that money will expect a return for having forgone an alternative use of these funds. This return is generally in the form of interest, which will accumulate at regular intervals, usually on an annual basis. The interest may be paid to the owner at regular intervals, and does not then itself accumulate interest. This is simple interest. The following example shows how simple interest is calculated.

Example. Calculate the simple interest on £70 for $3\frac{1}{2}$ years at 9 per cent.

Interest on £1 for 1 year is £0.09

Interest on £70 for 1 year is £(70 × 0.09)

Interest on £70 for $3\frac{1}{2}$ years is £(70 × 0.09 × 3.50)

$$= £22.05$$

Thus in general terms, if

P = the principal amount

i = rate of interest per annum expressed as a decimal

n = term of years

and I = total simple interest

then $I = P \times i \times n$

The reader may be acquainted with an alternative formula

$$I = \frac{P \times R \times T}{100}$$

where R = rate of interest per annum and T = term of years.

To calculate the total amount of original capital and interest, the principal amount is added to the total simple interest $(P + I)$.

The formula may be transposed to find the principal amount, the rate of interest per annum or the term of years. Thus

$$P = \frac{I}{i \times n}$$

$$i = \frac{I}{P \times n}$$

and

$$n = \frac{I}{P \times i}$$

Example. Calculate the amount which will have accumulated at the end of 5 years from a loan of £840 at $4\frac{1}{2}$ per cent simple interest.

In this example, P = £840, i = 0.045 and n = 5 years.

Amount accumulated $\;=\; P + I$

$=\; P + (P \times i \times n)$

$=\; 840 + (840 \times 0.045 \times 5)$

$=\; 840 + 189$

$=\; £1029$

Example. What sum would have to be invested at 9 per cent per annum rate of interest to provide an income of £500 per annum?

$i = 0.09$, $n = 1$ year and $I = £500$.

$$P = \frac{I}{i \times n}$$

$$= \frac{500}{0.09 \times 1}$$

$$= £5556$$

Example. Find the operative rate of simple interest per annum if £700 accumulates to £950 after 4 years.

$I = £950 - £700 = £250$, $P = £700$ and $n = 4$ years.

$$i = \frac{I}{P \times n}$$

$$= \frac{250}{700 \times 4}$$

$$= \frac{250}{2800}$$

$$= 0.089$$

$$= 9 \text{ per cent (approximately)}$$

Example. How many years does it take a sum of money to increase by 75 per cent when the rate of simple interest is $7\frac{1}{2}$ per cent per annum?

$I = 0.75P$ and $i = 0.075$.

$$n = \frac{I}{P \times i}$$

If $P = £1$, then

$$n = \frac{0.75}{1 \times 0.075}$$

$$= 10 \text{ years}$$

4.4 COMPOUND INTEREST

As previously stated, where money is invested, the investor will expect an annual return, that is, a rate of interest per annum. Instead of receiving a monetary return at regular intervals, he may choose to have the interest added to the principal amount. This interest, which will also accumulate further interest, is termed *compound interest*. A formula may be derived as follows.

Assume £1 is invested at i compound interest. At the end of the first year, £1 will accumulate to $(1 + i)$. At the end of the second year, it will accumulate to $(1 + i)i + (1 + i) = 1 + 2i + i^2 = (1 + i)^2$. At the end of the third year the sum will further accumulate to $(1 + 2i + i^2)i + (1 + 2i + i^2) = 1 + 3i + 3i^2 + i^3 = (i + i)^3$. So that at the end of n years, £1 will have accumulated to $£(1 + i)^n$. Thus

$$\text{total amount accumulated} = £(1 + i)^n$$

$$\text{and total interest} = £(1 + i)^n - 1$$

For the investment of a principal amount P and the total amount A

$$A = P(1 + i)^n$$

Example. To what amount will £750 accumulate after 5 years of $8\frac{1}{2}$ per cent compound interest?

$P = £750$, $n = 5$ years and $i = 0.085$.

$$A = P(1 + i)^n$$
$$A = 750 \times 1.085^5$$
$$= 750 \times 1.503$$
$$= £1127$$

The formula may be transposed to find the principal amount, the rate of interest per annum or term of years. Thus

$$P = \frac{A}{(1 + i)n}$$

$$i = \sqrt[n]{\frac{A}{P}} - 1$$

and

$$n = \frac{\log A - \log P}{\log (1 + i)}$$

Example. A man aged 57 years wishes to obtain a capital sum of £2000 on retirement in 8 years' time. What sum must he invest now at 9 per cent compound interest?

A = £2000, n = 8 years and i = 0.09.

$$P = \frac{A}{(1 + i)^n}$$

$$= \frac{2000}{1.09^8}$$

$$= \frac{2000}{1.993}$$

$$= £1004$$

Example. An investor wishes to double his capital after a period of 10 years. At what rate of compound interest per annum would he need to invest to achieve this?

A = $2P$ and n = 10 years

$$i = \sqrt[n]{\frac{A}{P}} - 1$$

$$= \sqrt[10]{\frac{2}{1}} - 1$$

$$= 1.072 - 1$$

$$= 0.072$$

$$= 7.2 \text{ per cent}$$

Example. A man has invested £1200 at $8\frac{1}{2}$ per cent compound interest. How long will it take for this amount to accumulate to £2000?

A = £2000, P = £1200 and i = 0.085.

$$n = \frac{\log A - \log P}{\log (1 + i)}$$

$$= \frac{\log 2000 - \log 1200}{\log 1.085}$$

$$= \frac{3.3010 - 3.0792}{0.0354}$$

$$= \frac{0.2218}{0.0354}$$

$$= 6.26 \text{ years}$$

4.5 MORTGAGE REPAYMENTS

If a capital sum of money is borrowed over a period of time, the lender may stipulate that repayment should be made at regular intervals during the period of borrowing, each repayment being of an equal amount. The agreement to lend and borrow capital for the purchase of land and/or property may be termed a *mortgage*; the borrower is called the *mortgagor*, and the lender the *mortgagee*.

Let the amount of the mortgage be M, and the annual repayment be P. If the mortgagee lends M for a period of n years, he releases not only M, but also the compound interest, at an annual rate of i, which would otherwise have accumulated each year, the total thus being $M(1 + i)^n$. The annual repayments P will also be able to accumulate compound interest at an annual rate of i.

The first payment of P will accumulate to $P(1 + i)^{n-1}$, the second payment of P to $P(1 + i)^{n-2}$, and so on. The sum of the repayments and interest will be $P(1 + i)^{n-1} + P(1 + i)^{n-2}$ and ... up to and including $P(1 + i)^2 + P(1 + i) + P$. If this is reversed, the sum of repayments and interest $= P + P(1 + i) + P(1 + i)^2 \ldots$ up to and including $P(1 + i)^{n-2} + P(1 + i)^{n-1}$.

This is a geometrical progression; the formula for the sum, provided earlier in this chapter, is

$$Sn = \frac{a(r^n - 1)}{r - 1}$$

where

Sn = the sum of repayments and interest

$a = P$

$r = (1 + i)$

Hence the sum of repayments and interest is

$$P \left[\frac{(1 + i)^n - 1}{(1 + i) - 1} \right]$$

$$= P \left[\frac{(1 + i)^n - 1}{i} \right]$$

The total of repayments and interest must equal the value of the mortgage with its interest. Thus

$$\frac{P((1 + i)^n - 1)}{i} = M(1 + i)^n$$

So

$$P = \frac{M(1 + i)^n \, i}{(1 + i)^n - 1}$$

Example. What would be the annual repayments on a mortgage of £4500 borrowed over 25 years at 11 per cent compound interest?

$$P = \frac{M(1 + i)^n \, i}{(1 + i)^n - 1}$$

where M = £4500, i = 0.11 and n = 25 years.

$$P = \frac{4500 \times 1.11^{25} \times 0.11}{1.11^{25} - 1}$$

$$P = \frac{4500 \times 13.57 \times 0.11}{13.57 - 1}$$

$$= \frac{6716}{12.57}$$

$$= £534.3$$

A mortgagor may decide that there is a maximum amount he can afford to pay in annual repayments, and he will wish to know the maximum amount, M, that he will be able to borrow. This can be found by transposing the formula

$$M = \frac{P((1 + i)^n - 1)}{(1 + i)^n i}$$

Example. A prospective mortgagor calculates that he can afford repayments totalling £250 per annum over a period of 25 years. If the borrowing rate is 10 per cent annum, what is the maximum amount he can borrow?

$$M = \frac{P((1 + i)^n - 1)}{(1 + i)^n i}$$

P = £250, i = 0.10 and n = 25 years. Thus

$$M = \frac{250 \times (1.10^{25} - 1)}{1.10^{25} \times 0.10}$$

$$= \frac{250 \times 9.84}{10.84 \times 0.10}$$

$$= \frac{2460}{1.084}$$

$$= £2270$$

Mortgages will be considered further in Chapter 5 when a mortgage instalment table will be analysed.

4.6   DEPRECIATION

When new plant or machinery is purchased, its value as at purchase will depreciate year by year. This annual depreciation may be expressed as a fixed percentage, i, per annum, when the value at any particular time can be determined by means of a compound interest calculation with a negative value. Thus, if the original value = P, the depreciating rate of interest per annum = i, term of years = n and the value after n years = D, then

$$D = P(1 - i)^n$$

Example. At the end of each year the depreciation of certain plant is taken as 8 per cent of its value at the beginning of the year. If the initial value is £3000, calculate the value after 7 years.

P = £3000, i = 0.08 and n = 7 years.

$$D = 3000 (1 - 0.08)^7$$

$$= 3000 \times 0.92^7$$

$$= £1674$$

Example. Equipment costs £500 when new. It is estimated that it depreciates in value by 10 per cent each year. In how many years (to the nearest year) will it be reduced to scrap value of £5?

P = £500, D = £5 and i = 0.10.

$$D = P(1 - i)^n$$

$$5 = 500(1 - 0.10)^n$$

$$5 = 500 \times 0.90^n$$

$$0.90^n = 0.01$$

$$\log 0.90 \times n = \log 0.01$$

$$n = \frac{\log 0.01}{\log 0.90} = \frac{\bar{2}.0000}{1.9542}$$

$$= \frac{-2}{-1 + 0.9542}$$

$$= \frac{-2}{-0.0458}$$

$$= 44 \text{ years}$$

QUESTIONS

4.1 What sum would have to be invested at 11 per cent per annum simple interest to provide an annual income of £750?

4.2 How many years will it take a sum of money to double itself when the rate of simple interest is 9 per cent per annum?

4.3 A man invests £250 at $9\frac{1}{2}$ per cent compound interest. To what amount will this accumulate at the end of 15 years?

4.4. A man wishes to provide a capital sum of £1500 in 10 years' time. What must he invest now if the compound interest rate is $8\frac{1}{2}$ per cent per annum?

4.5 An investor wishes to treble his capital over a period of 9 years. What rate of compound interest per annum would he require to achieve this?

4.6 Find the sum of the series $8 + 7.75 + 7.50 + \ldots + 0.25 + 0$.

4.7 Three numbers in an arithmetical progression have a product of 280 and a sum of 21. Find the numbers.

4.8 Find the sum of the first ten terms of the series $+ 12 - 6 + 3 \ldots$

4.9 What will be the annual repayments on a debt of £4000 borrowed over 30 years, if the compound interest rate is 8 per cent per annum?

4.10 A man wishes to borrow a capital sum but the maximum annual repayment he can afford to make over a 35 year period is £400. If the borrowing rate is 9 per cent per annum, what is the maximum amount he can borrow?

4.11 A builder buys a machine for £1000 and calculates depreciation at the rate of 13 per cent each year. In how many years will the machine be reduced to scrap value of £35?

4.12 A piece of machinery costs £1200 when new. It is estimated that it depreciates by 12 per cent per annum for the first three years and 10 per cent thereafter. What will be its value at the end of 10 years?

5 Construction and Analysis of Valuation Tables

In valuation and land use practice it is necessary to undertake calculations that are usually based upon compound interest principles. Valuation tables have been constructed to eliminate much of the time-consuming aspect of calculation work.

The tables to be studied in this chapter will be considered under three broad headings:

(1) Single Rate tables
(2) Dual Rate tables
(3) Mortgage Instalment table

The tables are based upon the £1 unit, unless specifically stated otherwise. The following abbreviations will be used:

i = rate of interest per annum expressed as a decimal
n = term of years (or number of periods of interest accumulation)
s = annual sinking fund to be invested to accumulate to £1 after a given number of years at a certain rate of compound interest.

The calculations in this chapter have been worked out using logarithms. The valuation tables are compiled with the use of a computer, so that there may be slight differences between the figures calculated from formulae and the valuation table figures.

5.1 SINGLE RATE TABLES

5.1.1 Amount of £1 (*A*)

This is the amount to which £1 invested now will accumulate at *i* compound interest in *n* years. It is assumed that interest is added annually at the end of each year. This is the compound interest table, and the formula was provided in Chapter 4.

$$A = (1 + i)^n$$

Example. To what amount will £1 invested at 6 per cent compound interest accumulate in 4 years?

$$A = (1 + i)^n$$
$$= (1 + 0.06)^4$$
$$= 1.06^4$$
$$= £1.263$$

The table assumes that the compound interest will be added annually; there will be many instances where interest is payable at intervals less than this, such as half-yearly, quarterly and monthly. The formula may be adjusted to take account of this, by observing the following rules.

   (i) divide *i* by the number of interest accumulations in the year
   (ii) multiply *n* by the number of interest accumulations in the year

If the interest is accumulating half-yearly, the formula becomes

$$A = \left(1 + \frac{i}{2}\right)^{2n}$$

and quarterly

$$A = \left(1 + \frac{i}{4}\right)^{4n}$$

Referring to the previous example, to what amount will £1 invested at 6 per cent accumulate in 4 years

(i) if interest is payable half-yearly?
(ii) if interest is payable quarterly?

(i) $A = \left(1 + \dfrac{i}{2}\right)^{2n}$

$\qquad = 1.03^8$

$\qquad = £1.266$

(Valuation tables give a figure of 1.2668.)

(ii) $A = \left(1 + \dfrac{i}{4}\right)^{4n}$

$\qquad = 1.015^{16}$

$\qquad = £1.266$

(Valuation tables give a figure of 1.2690.)

Example. To what amount will £100 invested at 15 per cent rate of interest accumulate in 8 years, if interest is payable monthly?

$A = \left(1 + \dfrac{i}{12}\right)^{12n}$

$\quad = \left(1 + \dfrac{0.15}{12}\right)^{12 \times 8}$

$\quad = 1.0125^{96}$

$\quad = 3.227$

(Valuation tables give a figure of 3.2955.) For £100

$A = 3.227 \times 100$

$\quad = £323$

The Amount of £1 table forms the basis for all subsequent valuation tables.

5.1.2 Present Value of £1 (PV)

This is the amount that must be invested now to accumulate to £1 at *i* compound interest in *n* years. The formula for this table may be constructed as follows

(i) Assume £1 is invested at *i* for 1 year; then at the end of the year the accumulation will be £$(1 + i)$.

(ii) Assume *x* (an unknown) is invested at *i* for 1 year, and at the end of the year the accumulation will be £1.

In (i) £1 is the Present Value (PV). In (ii) *x* is the Present Value (PV).

$$x : 1 = 1 : 1 + i$$

so that

$$x = \frac{1}{1 + i}$$

Thus

$$PV = \frac{1}{(1 + i)^n}$$

This is the reciprocal of the Amount of £1 table.

Example. What amount must be invested now at 8 per cent to accumulate to £1 in 7 years' time?

$$PV = \frac{1}{(1 + i)^n}$$

$$\frac{1}{1.08^7} = \frac{1}{1.713}$$

$$= £0.583$$

The Present Value of £1 table gives the current value of the right to receive £1 at a known future date. This Present Value is termed the *deferred value* of a future sum. The table may also be used to calculate the capital sum to be invested now to provide for a known future liability.

Example. A man has the right to receive £1000 in 12 years' time. What is the present value of this right, assuming that capital could be invested at $7\frac{1}{2}$ per cent compound interest?

$$PV = \frac{1}{(1 + i)^n}$$

$$= \frac{1}{1.075^{12}}$$

$$= \frac{1}{2.381}$$

$$= 0.419$$

For £1000

$$PV = 0.419 \times £1000 = £419$$

Example. The owner of a house anticipates that he will need to renew a roof at an estimated cost of £850 in 6 years' time. Assuming that capital could be invested at $9\frac{1}{4}$ per cent compound interest, what must he invest now to meet his future liability (ignoring inflation)?

$$PV \text{ of } £1 = \frac{1}{(1 + i)^n}$$

$$= \frac{1}{1.0925^6}$$

$$= \frac{1}{1.7} = 0.588$$

For £850

$$PV = 0.588 \times £850$$
$$= £499.8$$

5.1.3 The Amount of £1 per Annum

This is the amount to which £1 invested at the end of each year will accumulate at i compound interest in n years. The formula for this table is compiled as follows.

If interest is not paid until the end of the first year, the first £1 invested will accumulate for $(n - 1)$ years and the second £1 for $(n - 2)$ years; this pattern will continue until the investment of the last £1, which will gain no interest. Hence the amount of £1 per annum $= (1 + i)^{n-1} + (1 + i)^{n-2} \ldots$ up to and including $(1 + i)^2 + (1 + i) + 1$.

If these terms are reversed for convenience, then the amount of £1 per annum $= 1 + (1 + i) + (1 + i)^2 \ldots$ up to and including $(1 + i)^{n-1}$.

This series of terms is geometrical progression and it was shown in Chapter 3 that the general expression for the sum of such terms is

$$Sn = \frac{a(r^n - 1)}{r - 1}$$

In this series Sn may be substituted by the amount of £1 per annum; a by 1; r by $(1 + i)$ so that

$$\text{Amount of £1 per annum} = \frac{1(1 + i)^n - 1}{(1 + i) - 1}$$

$$= \frac{(1 + i)^n - 1}{i} \text{ or } \frac{A - 1}{i}$$

(where A = amount of £1.)

Example. £100 is invested at the end of each year in a building society giving $6\frac{1}{2}$ per cent compound interest. To what amount will this accumulate after 20 years?

$$\text{Amount of £1 per annum} = \frac{(1 + i)^n - 1}{i}$$

$$= \frac{1.065^{20} - 1}{0.065}$$

$$= \frac{3.516 - 1}{0.065} = \frac{2.516}{0.065}$$

$$= 38.7$$

(Valuation tables give a figure of 38.8253.) For £100, accumulation will be

$$38.7 \times £100 = £3870$$

This table is therefore derived from the addition of the amounts of £1 for each £1 invested over the period of n years.

Example. Calculate the Amount of £1 per annum for 3 years at 6 per cent compound interest.

(i) By the addition of the Amounts of £1

$$(1 + i)^{n-1} + (1 + i)^{n-2} + 1$$

$$= 1.06^2 + 1.06^1 + 1$$

$$= 1.123 + 1.06 + 1$$

$$= 3.183$$

(ii) By using the formula $[(1 + i)^n - 1]/i$

$$= \frac{(1.06)^3 - 1}{0.06}$$

$$= \frac{1.191 - 1}{0.06} = \frac{0.191}{0.06}$$

$$= 3.183$$

5.1.4 Annual Sinking Fund (s)

This is the annual sum, s, required to be invested at the end of each year to accumulate to £1 in n years at i compound interest.

Since the Present Value of £1 is the reciprocal of the Amount of £1, so the Annual Sinking Fund is the reciprocal of the Amount of £1 per annum. The formula is

$$s = \frac{i}{(1 + i)^n - 1} \text{ or } \frac{i}{A - 1}$$

The Annual Sinking Fund may be used to calculate the annual amount to be set aside to meet a known future liability or expense.

Example. The owner of a house anticipates that he will need to provide a new staircase in 10 years' time at an estimated cost of £700. If capital can be invested at 8 per cent compound interest, what amount should be invested annually to meet his future liability?

$$s = \frac{i}{(1 + i)^n - 1}$$

$$= \frac{0.08}{1.08^{10} - 1}$$

$$= \frac{0.08}{2.158 - 1} = \frac{0.08}{1.158}$$

$$= 0.069$$

So that the Annual Sinking Fund to provide £700

$$= 0.069 \times £700$$

$$= £48.3$$

The formula assumes that the sinking fund payment would be made at the end of the year. Where payments have to be made at the beginning of each year, the formula would be adjusted to

$$\frac{i}{(1 + i)^{n + 1} - 1}$$

Example. Calculate the Annual Sinking Fund to produce £1 in 21 years at 7 per cent assuming the payment will be made (i) at the beginning of each year, and (ii) at the end of each year.

(i) $$s = \frac{i}{(1 + i)^{n + 1} - 1}$$

$$= \frac{0.07}{1.07^{22} - 1}$$

$$= \frac{0.07}{4.43 - 1} = \frac{0.07}{3.43}$$

$$= 0.0204$$

(ii) $$s = \frac{i}{(1 + i)^n - 1}$$

$$= \frac{0.07}{1.07^{21} - 1}$$

$$= \frac{0.07}{4.14 - 1} = \frac{0.07}{3.14}$$

$$= 0.022$$

5.1.5 Years' Purchase (YP) or Present Value of £1 per Annum

This is the present value of the right to receive £1 at the end of each year for *n* years at *i* compound interest. The formula is derived from the addition of the Present Values of £1 for each £1 received. Thus

PV of £1 due in 1 year $= \dfrac{1}{1 + i}$

PV of £1 due in 2 years $= \dfrac{1}{(1 + i)^2}$

Years' Purchase for 2 years $= \dfrac{1}{1 + i} + \dfrac{1}{(1 + i)^2}$

Thus

Years' Purchase for *n* years $= \dfrac{1}{1 + i} + \dfrac{1}{(1 + i)^2} + \dfrac{1}{(1 + i)^3} \cdots$

up to and including $\dfrac{1}{(1 + i)^{n-1}} + \dfrac{1}{(1 + i)^n}$

Multiply both sides by $(1 + i)$ and call the resultant equation (5.2).

Years' Purchase for *n* years $\times (1 + i) = \dfrac{1 + i}{1 + i} + \dfrac{1 + i}{(1 + i)^2}$

$$+ \dfrac{1 + i}{(1 + i)^3} \cdots$$

up to and including $\dfrac{1 + i}{(1 + i)^{n-1}} + \dfrac{1 + i}{(1 + i)^n}$ (5.2)

This can be expressed as

Years' Purchase for *n* years $\times (1 + i) = 1 + \dfrac{1}{1 + i} + \dfrac{1}{(1 + i)^2} \cdots$

up to and including $\dfrac{1}{(1 + i)^{n-2}} + \dfrac{1}{(1 + i)^{n-1}}$

Subtract equation 5.1 from equation 5.2 giving the Years' Purchase for n years $\times (1 + i)$ − the Years' Purchase for n years as

$$1 - \frac{1}{(1 + i)^n}$$

This is Years' Purchase for n years + i (Years' Purchase for n years) − Years' Purchase for n years which equals

$$1 - \frac{1}{(1 + i)^n}$$

$$i \text{ (Years' Purchase for } n \text{ years)} = 1 - \frac{1}{(1 + i)^n}$$

Years' Purchase for n years (YP) $= \dfrac{1 - \dfrac{1}{(1 + i)^n}}{i}$ or $\dfrac{1 - PV}{i}$

(where PV = Present Value of £1.)

This table gives the multiplier which can be applied to an income receivable at the end of each year for n years at i compound interest in order to find its present capital value.

Example. A landlord will receive £100 per annum rent from his tenant for the next 20 years. Assuming 8 per cent compound interest, what is the capital value of the income?

$$\text{YP for 20 years at 8 per cent} = \frac{1 - \dfrac{1}{(1 + i)^n}}{i}$$

$$= \frac{1 - \dfrac{1}{1.08^{20}}}{0.08}$$

$$= \frac{1 - \dfrac{1}{4.66}}{0.08} = \frac{1 - 0.2145}{0.08}$$

$$= \frac{0.7855}{0.08}$$

$$= 9.818$$

So that

    capital value of £100 per annum $= 9.818 \times £100$

$$= £981.8$$

This may be more conveniently set out as follows

    rent received per annum   £100

    YP for 20 years at 8 per cent   <u>9.818</u>

            Capital value $=$ £981.8

The use of a single-rate YP table assumes that the income being valued will be followed by another stream of income (see section on Dual rate tables).

5.1.6 Years' Purchase in Perpetuity (YP)

This is the present value of the right to receive £1 at the end of each year in perpetuity at i compound interest. This differs from the previous table in that the income is received not for a limited period of time but for perpetuity, that is, an endless period of time. If the inome at the end of each year is £1, and the investor requires a return (or *net income*) of say 8 per cent (i) then £1 is 8 per cent of the capital value. So that

$$\text{YP} = \frac{1}{0.08} = 12.5 \text{ giving the formula}$$

$$\text{YP in perpetuity} = \frac{1}{i}$$

This YP can be multiplied to any perpetual income receivable at the end of each year at i compound interest.

Example. A is the owner of a freehold interest in a shop yielding a net income at £250 per annum. Assuming 7 per cent compound interest, calculate the capital value of A's interest.

Net income per annum = £250

YP in perpetuity at 7 per cent $= \dfrac{1}{i} = \dfrac{1}{0.07} = \underline{14.286}$

Capital value = £3571

5.1.7 Years' Purchase of a Reversion to a Perpetuity

This is the present value of the right to receive £1 at the end of each year in perpetuity at i compound interest, but receivable after the expiration of n years.

It has been established that, if £1 is receivable at the end of each year in perpetuity, then its capital value (YP) = $1/i$. However, this YP would not be paid for a stream of income that was not receivable until n years had expired. The present value of such income would be the amount that could be invested now at i to produce $1/i$ in n years; this is the PV of $1/i$.

The YP of a reversion to a perpetuity is given by

$$\text{PV of £1} \times \frac{1}{i}$$

$$= \frac{1}{(1 + i)^n} \times \frac{1}{i}$$

$$= \frac{1}{i(1 + i)^n} \text{ or } \frac{1}{iA}$$

Example. What is the capital value of the right to receive £1 per annum in perpetuity commencing in 7 years' time? (Assume 7 per cent compound interest.)

$$YP = \frac{1}{i(1 + i)^n}$$

$$= \frac{1}{0.07 \times 1.07^7}$$

$$= \frac{1}{0.07 \times 1.606} = \frac{1}{0.1124}$$

$$= 8.896$$

This would be set out as follows

Net income per annum $\qquad$ = £1

YP in perpetuity at 7 per cent $= \dfrac{1}{i}$

$$= \dfrac{1}{0.07} = 14.286$$

PV of £1 for 7 years at 7 per cent

$$= \dfrac{1}{(1 + i)^n} = \dfrac{1}{1.07^7} \qquad = \underline{0.6227}$$

YP in perpetuity deferred 7 years at 7 per cent = <u>8.896</u>

Capital value = £8.896

This table will be used for the valuation of reversions in freehold interests.

Example. The owner of freehold property will receive net income of £275 per annum, commencing in 4 years' time. Assuming a return of 8 per cent, value his interest.

Net income per annum $\qquad$ = £275

YP in perpetuity deferred 4 years at 8 per cent

$$= \dfrac{1}{i(1 + i)^n}$$

$$= \dfrac{1}{0.08 \times 1.08^4} = \dfrac{1}{0.08 \times 1.36}$$

$$= \dfrac{1}{0.109} \qquad = \underline{9.18}$$

Capital value = £2524

5.1.8 Interest at Intervals of Less than One Year

The Single Rate tables analysed in this chapter have been based on the assumption that the interest would accumulate at annual intervals. Interest may accumulate at periods less than the year such as half-yearly, quarterly and monthly; this was considered earlier in this chapter with the Amount of £1. The rule in these situations is

(i) Divide i by the number of interest accumulations in the year
(ii) Multiply n by the number of interest accumulations in the year

In the same way, other tables may be modified.

Example. Find the capital value of an income of £200 per annum for 12 years at 8 per cent compound interest.

Income per annum =   £200

YP for 12 years at 8 per cent

$$= \frac{1 - \dfrac{1}{(1 + i)^n}}{i} = \frac{1 - \dfrac{1}{1.08^{12}}}{0.08}$$

$$= \frac{1 - 0.397}{0.08} = \frac{0.603}{0.08} = \underline{7.54}$$

Capital Value = £1508

If the interest were credited half-yearly, there would be 24 separate incomes of £100 each at 4 per cent compound interest for each half-year. The amended calculation would be

Net income per period = £100

YP for 24 periods at 4 per cent per period

$$= \frac{1 - \dfrac{1}{(1 + i)^n}}{i} = \frac{1 - \dfrac{1}{1.04^{24}}}{0.04}$$

$$= \frac{1 - 0.39}{0.04} \quad = \frac{0.61}{0.04} = \underline{15.25}$$

Capital value = £1525

5.1.9 Income to be Received at Intervals of more than One Year

There may be circumstances where income is received not at the end of each year but at greater intervals. The capital value may be calculated by using the formula

capital value = amount of each payment ×

$$\left(\frac{\text{YP for the total term}}{\text{YP for period between payments}} \right) \times \begin{array}{l} \text{PV of £1 for period before} \\ \text{receipt of first payment} \end{array}$$

Example. What is the capital value of the right to receive 5 payments each of £100, these being received at 5 years intervals? (Assume 8 per cent compound interest.)

Each payment = £100

$$\frac{\text{YP for the total term}}{\text{YP for period between payments}} \times \begin{array}{l} \text{PV of £1 for period before} \\ \text{receipt of first payment} \end{array}$$

$$= \frac{\text{YP for 25 years at 8 per cent}}{\text{YP for five years at 8 per cent}} \times \begin{array}{l} \text{PV of £1 for 5 years at 8} \\ \text{per cent} \end{array}$$

$$= \frac{10.67}{3.99} \times 0.681 \qquad\qquad = \underline{1.821}$$

Capital value = £182.1

The parts of the formula are calculated as follows.

$$\text{YP for 25 years at 8 per cent} = \frac{1 - \dfrac{1}{1.08^{25}}}{0.08} = \frac{1 - 0.1462}{0.08}$$

$$= 10.67$$

$$\text{YP for 5 years at 8 per cent} = \frac{1 - \dfrac{1}{1.08^5}}{0.08} = \frac{1 - 0.681}{0.08}$$

$$= 3.99$$

$$\text{PV of £1 for 5 years at 8 per cent} = \frac{1}{1.08^5} = 0.681$$

Without using the formula, the answer could be established as follows

Each payment	= £100
PV of £1 for 5 years at 8 per cent	= 0.681
10 years at 8 per cent	= 0.463
15 years at 8 per cent	= 0.316
20 years at 8 per cent	= 0.215
25 years at 8 per cent	= 0.146
	= 1.821

Capital value = £182.1

QUESTIONS

Without the use of valuation tables, evaluate the following.

5.1 The Amount of £1 for 15 years at 9 per cent compound interest.

5.2 The Present Value of £1 for 14 years at $7\frac{1}{2}$ per cent compound interest.

5.3 The capital value of the right to receive £150 per annum for 8 years at $8\frac{1}{2}$ per cent compound interest.

5.4 The Annual Sinking fund to produce £250 in 16 years at 6 per cent compound interest.

5.5 The capital value of a freehold interest in property yielding a net income of £225 per annum. The income will commence in 5 years' time. Assume 8 per cent compound interest.

5.6 The present liability to an owner of property, who anticipates he will need to spend £200 in 5 years' time to repair staircase and a further £500 in 8 years' time to carry out roof repairs.

Assume that capital could be invested at 6 per cent compound interest.

5.2 DUAL RATE TABLES

5.2.1 Years' Purchase or Present Value of £1 per Annum (YP)

This is the capital value of the right to receive £1 at the end of each year for *n* years at *i* compound interest, but allowing for a sinking fund *s* to recoup the original capital after 'n' years.

Dual Rate tables should be used for calculating the capital value of income that is to be received for a known limited period. This will occur in land and property with leasehold interests that will expire on a specified date.

If an interest has income that is receivable for a limited period only, the purchaser could not afford to pay the same amount as for the purchasing of a perpetual stream of income. At the end of the period the income would cease and the original capital (purchase price) would be lost. Dual Rate tables are based on the assumption that the investor would annually set aside a sum out of the income received. This would be invested as a sinking fund to recoup the original capital at the end of the term. The Years' Purchase must reflect the fact that the investor has a lower *spendable income* than in the case of the perpetual income.

Example. What is the capital value of £100 per annum receivable in perpetuity? The owner requires an 8 per cent return.

Net income per annum　　　　= £100

YP in perpetuity at 8 per cent

$$= \frac{1}{i} = \frac{1}{0.08} \qquad = \underline{12.5}$$

Capital value = £1250

If the stream of income is receivable for 25 years only, then the capital value could be calculated as follows.

Assume the capital value to be *x*. The sinking fund to recoup *x* at the end of 25 years should be invested at a risk-free net rate of interest such as $2\frac{1}{2}$ per cent. (This is referred to as an *accumulative* rate of interest.) Hence

Net income per annum = £100

Less s to recoup £1 in 25 years at $2\frac{1}{2}$ per cent

$$= \frac{i}{(1 + i)^n - 1} = \frac{0.025}{1.02525 - 1} = 0.029$$

s to recoup x in 25 years at $2\frac{1}{2}$ per cent = $\underline{0.029x}$

Spendable income per annum	= $100 - 0.029x$
YP in perpetuity at 8 per cent	= 12.5
Capital value	= $1250 - 0.3625x$

The capital value is x, thus

$$1250 - 0.3625x = x$$
$$1250 = 1.3625x$$
$$x = \frac{1250}{1.3625}$$

Capital value = £917

This capital value could have been calculated by using the Dual Rate YP table, which is constructed as follows.

Assume the net interest on £1 to be i and the annual sinking fund to recoup £1 at the end of the limited term to be s. Then the total income from property worth a capital value of £1 = $i + s$. Assume the capital value of a stream of income to be P. Then the annual income required is $P(i + s)$. But

Capital value = Net income per annum × YP

So that

$$YP = \frac{P}{P(i + s)}$$

$$YP = \frac{1}{i + s}$$

In this formula, there are two different rates of interest

(i) i is the rate of interest expected by the investor (known as a *remunerative* rate of interest).

(ii) the rate of interest for s is a low, risk-free rate (an *accumulative* rate of interest).

Referring to the previous example of income of £100 per annum receivable for 25 years only, this can now be calculated using the Dual Rate YP formula.

Net income per annum $= £100$

YP for 25 years at 8 per cent and $2\frac{1}{2}$ per cent

$$= \frac{1}{i + s} = \frac{1}{i + \dfrac{i}{(1 + i)^n - 1}}$$

$$= \frac{1}{0.08 + \dfrac{0.025}{1.025^{25} - 1}}$$

$$= \frac{1}{0.08 + 0.029}$$

$$= \frac{1}{0.109} \qquad\qquad = \underline{9.17}$$

Capital value $= £917$

Example. What is the capital value of an income of £500 per annum receivable for 12 years only? The investor requires an 8 per cent return.

Net income per annum $= £500$

YP for 12 years at 8 per cent and $2\frac{1}{2}$ per cent

$$= \frac{1}{i + s} = \frac{1}{i + \dfrac{i}{(1 + i)^n - 1}}$$

$$= \frac{1}{0.08 + \dfrac{0.025}{1.025^{12} - 1}}$$

$$= \frac{1}{0.08 + 0.0726}$$

$$= \frac{1}{0.1526} \qquad\qquad = \underline{6.553}$$

Capital value = £3276

This can be checked as follows.

Net income per annum $\qquad\qquad$ = £500

Less s to recoup £3276 in 12 years at $2\frac{1}{2}$ per cent

$= 0.0726 \times 3276$ $\qquad\qquad$ = $\underline{237.83}$

Spendable income per annum $\qquad\qquad$ £262.17

YP in perpetuity at 8 per cent $\qquad\qquad$ $\underline{12.5}$

Capital value $\qquad\qquad$ = £3277

(The £1 discrepancy has occurred because of the 'rounding-off' of figures.)

Referring to an earlier section of this chapter, the Single Rate YP was calculated from the formula

$$\frac{1 - \dfrac{1}{(1 + i)^n}}{i}$$

It may appear that this does not incorporate a sinking fund element as in the Dual Rate YP. However, Dual Rate tables could be used in a Single Rate situation, but the rate of interest to be used for the sinking fund element would be the same as for i, the remunerative rate of interest.

Example. Calculate the YP (Single Rate) for 10 years at 6 per cent.

Using the Single Rate formula

$$YP = \frac{1 - \dfrac{1}{(1 + i)^n}}{i}$$

$$= \frac{1 - \dfrac{1}{1.06^{10}}}{0.06}$$

$$= \frac{1 - 0.5583}{0.06} = \frac{0.4417}{0.06}$$

$$= 7.36$$

Using the Dual Rate formula

$$YP = \frac{1}{i + s} = \frac{1}{i + \dfrac{i}{(1 + i)^n - 1}}$$

$$= \frac{1}{0.06 + \dfrac{0.06}{1.06^{10} - 1}}$$

$$= \frac{1}{0.06 + 0.0758} = \frac{1}{0.1358}$$

$$= 7.36$$

5.2.2 The Effect of Tax on the Sinking Fund Element of the Dual Rate YP

No reference has been made in earlier sections of this chapter to the effect of tax on incomes being received. The net income receivable from property (that is, rent) is normally taxable. It is often considered that the tax is on the person and not the property, so that the tax on income is often ignored in the calculation of capital values.

However, in the dual rate calculation, a proportion of income is assumed to be set aside for the provision of a sinking fund. This sinking fund has been allocated in the case of the leasehold interest because the income is for a limited period and is subject to tax. Not only is the sinking fund element (the amount set aside annually) taxed, but also the interest, which accumulates each year. The Dual Rate YP formula must be adjusted to take account of this tax liability.

The accumulative rate of interest must be incorporated in the formula as a net rate of interest adjusted for tax. A gross rate of interest may be reduced to a net figure by multiplying by the net adjustment factor, T_N, where

$$T_N = 1 - x$$

where

$$x = \frac{\text{Rate of tax (new pence)}}{100}$$

For example, if

Gross rate of interest $= 4\frac{1}{2}$ per cent

Tax liability $\qquad = 30p$ in £

Then

Net rate of interest $=$ Gross rate $\times (1 - x)$

$$= 4\tfrac{1}{2} \times (1 - \tfrac{30}{100})$$

$$= 4\tfrac{1}{2} \times \tfrac{70}{100}$$

$$= 3.15 \text{ per cent}$$

The net interest rate usually used in the formula is $2\frac{1}{2}$ or 3 per cent.
    The sinking fund element s must be increased by multiplying by the gross adjustment factor T_G, where

$$T_G = \frac{1}{1 - x}$$

So that the sinking fund element becomes

$$s \left(\frac{1}{1 - x} \right)$$

The adjusted formula is

$$YP = \frac{1}{i + s \left(\dfrac{1}{1 - x} \right)}$$

A problem in ascertaining capital values may be that different investors have differing tax responsibilities. If no specific information is given, it is usual when using the formula to take the basic rate of tax for x. A typical tax rate is 33 per cent.

Example. What is the capital value of an income of £500 per annum receivable for 12 years only? An investor will require an 8 per cent return and a sinking fund could be invested at $4\frac{1}{4}$ per cent gross.

$$\text{Net interest for } s = \text{Gross interest} \times (1 - x)$$

$$= 4\frac{1}{4} \times (1 + \tfrac{33}{100})$$

$$= 4\frac{1}{4} \times \tfrac{67}{100}$$

$$= 2.847 \text{ per cent}$$

(Say, 3 per cent since valuation tables are worked for the nearest $\frac{1}{2}$ per cent.) Then

Net income per annum $\qquad\qquad\qquad\qquad\qquad$ = £500

YP for 12 years at 8 per cent and 3 per cent net (tax 33p in £)

$$= \frac{1}{i + s\left(\dfrac{1}{1 - x}\right)}$$

$$= \frac{1}{0.08 + \left(\dfrac{0.03}{1.03^{12} - 1} \times \dfrac{1}{0.67}\right)}$$

$$= \frac{1}{0.08 + \left(0.071 \times \dfrac{1}{0.67}\right)}$$

$$= \frac{1}{0.08 + 0.1059} = \frac{1}{0.1859} \qquad\qquad = \underline{5.379}$$

$$\text{Capital value} \qquad\qquad\qquad = \text{£2690}$$

This can be checked as follows.

Net income per annum   = £500

Less *s* to recoup £2690 in 12 years time at 3 per cent net

= 0.071 × 2690 = 190.99

Tax at 33p in £ on *s*

= (0.1059 − 0.071) 2690 = 0.0349 × 2690 = <u>93.88</u> <u>£284.87</u>

Spendable income per annum   £215.13

YP in perpetuity at 8 per cent   = <u>12.5</u>

Capital value   = £2690

5.2.3 The Annuity £1 will Purchase

This is the annual income receivable at the end of each year for *n* years if £1 is invested at *i* compound interest and a sinking fund is provided at $2\frac{1}{2}$ per cent to recoup the £1 at the end of the term. It is the reciprocal of the YP Dual Rate table. Hence

Annuity £1 will purchase = $i + s$

An alternative name is the Annual Equivalent.

Example. A purchaser recently bought an interest for £20 000; it had 15 years' duration. If he required a 7 per cent return, what was the net income per annum receivable from the property?

Net income per annum = Capital value x $(i + s)$

$$= 20\,000 \times \left(0.07 + \frac{0.025}{1.025^{15} - 1}\right)$$

$$= 20\,000 \times (0.07 + 0.056)$$

$$= 20\,000 \times 0.126$$

$$= £2520$$

This could have been calculated by dividing the capital value by the YP

£20 000
___

YP for 15 years at 7 per cent and $2\frac{1}{2}$ per cent

$= \dfrac{20\,000}{7.936}$

$= £2520$

There is, also, an Annuity £1 will purchase table on a Single Rate basis. This allows for the sinking fund to accumulate at the same rate as that which is required on the invested capital.

Taking the previous example, if the sinking fund were invested at 7 per cent

Net income per annum $= £20\,000 \times (i + s)$

$= 20\,000 \times \left(0.07 + \dfrac{0.07}{1.07^{15} - 1}\right)$

$= 20\,000 \times (0.07 + 0.0397)$

$= 20\,000 \times 0.1097$

$= £2194$

5.3 INTERNAL RATE OF RETURN TABLES

These tables are considered in Chapter 6.

QUESTIONS

5.7 Calculate the YP Dual Rate for 15 years at 9 per cent and 3 per cent net (tax 33p in £).

5.8 An investor receives an income of £500 per annum from an interest for 25 years only. Calculate the capital value, assuming he requires a yield of 10 per cent. A sinking fund could be invested at 5 per cent gross, and the investor's tax liability is 33p in £.

5.9 An income of £1 per annum receivable for 32 years is worth £8. If a sinking fund can be invested at $2\frac{1}{2}$ per cent net and tax is 40 p in £, what is the yield?

5.10 An income of £750 per annum is receivable for 19 years only.

Assuming a yield of 7 per cent and a sinking fund of $2\frac{1}{2}$ per cent net, calculate the capital value of the income if (i) there is no allowance for tax, and (ii) there is an allowance of 40p in £ for tax.

5.11 A purchaser recently bought an interest, which had 10 years' duration, for £12 300. If he required an 8 per cent return, what was the net income per annum receivable from the property? (Ignore tax.)

5.4 MORTGAGE INSTALMENT TABLE

This indicates the equal amounts to be paid monthly to redeem each £100 capital borrowed over *n* years at *i* compound interest. It is calculated on a fixed annual basis with no allowance for interest to compound on each monthly instalment.

It is an extension on a Single Rate basis of the Annuity £1 will purchase formula.

The Mortgage Instalment table is computed from

$$\frac{(i + s)\ 100}{12}$$

Example. Calculate the monthly instalment to redeem £3000 borrowed over 25 years at $10\frac{1}{2}$ per cent compound interest.

Capital sum per annum = £3000

Mortgage redemption for £3000

$$= 30 \times \frac{(i + s)\ 100}{12}$$

$$= 30 \times \frac{\left(0.105 + \dfrac{0.105}{1.105^{25} - 1}\right) 100}{12}$$

$$= 30 \times \frac{0.114 \times 100}{12}$$

$$= 30 \times 0.95$$

$$= £28.5 \text{ per month}$$

An alternative formula was used when mortgages were considered in Chapter 4. This was

$$P = \frac{M(1 + i)^n i}{(1 + i)^n - 1}$$

Taking the previous example

$$P = \frac{3000 \times (1.105)^{25} \times 0.105}{1.105^{25} - 1}$$

$$= \frac{3000 \times 12.16 \times 0.105}{11.16}$$

$$= £343.22 \text{ per annum}$$

This gives a monthly payment of £28.6.

It is possible to calculate the amount of capital outstanding at a particular time by multiplying the annual repayment by the Years' Purchase for the unexpended term of the borrowing period.

Example. In the previous example £3000 was borrowed over 25 years at $10\frac{1}{2}$ per cent, compound interest. The annual repayment was £343.22. What capital would be outstanding after 10 years?

Capital outstanding = Annual repayment × YP for the
unexpired term

$$343.22 \times \frac{1}{i + s}$$

$$= 343.22 \times \frac{1}{\left(0.105 + \dfrac{0.105}{1.105^{15} - 1}\right)}$$

$$= 343.22 \times \frac{1}{0.105 + 0.0303}$$

$$= 343.22 \times 7.39$$

$$= £2536$$

QUESTIONS

5.12 Calculate the monthly instalments to redeem £2000 to be repaid over 20 years at $8\frac{1}{2}$ per cent compound interest.

5.13 A borrower can afford a mortgage repayment of £25 per month. If he wishes to redeem capital over 18 years at $9\frac{1}{2}$ per cent compound interest what is the maximum amount he can borrow?

5.5 VALUATION FORMULAE AND THEIR INTER-RELATIONSHIP

Many examinations in the subject of valuation will include questions designed to test the candidate's knowledge of valuation formulae and how they relate. Such questions may take the following form.

Example. Given that the PV of £1 in 20 years at 5 per cent = 0.377, calculate the YP Single Rate for 20 years at 5 per cent.

The formula for YP Single Rate is

$$\frac{1 - PV}{i}$$

It is given that the PV of £1 for 20 years at 5 per cent is 0.377, hence

$$\text{YP for 20 years at 5 per cent} = \frac{1 - 0.377}{0.05} = \frac{0.623}{0.05}$$

$$= 12.46$$

There may be information given that cannot always be directly substituted into another formula.

Example. Given that the Annual Sinking fund to replace £1 in 21 years at $2\frac{1}{2}$ per cent is 0.037, calculate the Present Value of £1 in 21 years at $2\frac{1}{2}$ per cent.

It can be seen that the Annual Sinking fund cannot be substituted directly into the PV formula to give the required answer. The formulae for the two should be considered and the common factor found.

$$s = \frac{i}{A - 1}$$

and

$$PV = \frac{1}{A}$$

A is the factor common to both formulae, so that the question should be answered thus

Given that *s* to replace £1 in 21 years at $2\frac{1}{2}$ per cent is 0.037, then

$$0.037 = \frac{i}{1 - A}$$

$$0.037 = \frac{0.025}{A - 1}$$

$$A = \frac{0.025}{0.037} + 1 = 1.68$$

But

$$PV = \frac{1}{A} = \frac{1}{1.68} = 0.595$$

So that

PV of £1 for 21 years at $2\frac{1}{2}$ per cent = 0.595

The answer to this type of example could be found by using the appropriate formula, without reference to the given information. The function of this type of question, however, is to establish how the formulae have been derived and how they are interdependent. Further examples will illustrate this.

Example. Given that the PV of £1 for 10 years at 5 per cent = 0.614, calculate the Amount of £1 per annum for 8 years at 5 per cent.

$$PV = \frac{1}{A}$$

$$\text{Amount of £1 per annum} = \frac{A - 1}{i}$$

So that the common factor is A. PV of £1 = 0.614 = 1/A, then

$$A \text{ for 10 years at 5 per cent} = \frac{1}{PV}$$

$$= 1.63$$

$$A \text{ for 8 years at 5 per cent} = \frac{A \text{ for 10 years}}{A \text{ for 2 years}}$$

$$= \frac{1.63}{(1 + i)^2} = \frac{1.63}{1.05^2}$$

$$= \frac{1.63}{1.10} = 1.48$$

So that

Amount of £1 per annum for 8 years at 5 per cent

$$= \frac{A - 1}{i} = \frac{1.48 - 1}{0.05} = \frac{0.48}{0.05}$$

$$= 9.6$$

Example. Calculate the PV of £1 in 3 years at 8 per cent, given that the PV of £1 in 1 year at 8 per cent is 0.926 and the Single Rate YP for 2 years at 8 per cent is 1.783.

$$\text{Single Rate YP} = \frac{1 - PV}{i}$$

$$1.783 = \frac{1 - PV \text{ for 2 years at 8 per cent}}{0.08}$$

$$1.783 \times 0.08 = 1 - PV \text{ for 2 years at 8 per cent}$$

$$PV \text{ for 2 years at 8 per cent} = 1 - (1.783 \times 0.08)$$

$$= 1 - 0.14264 = 0.85736 = 0.8574$$

But PV of £1 for 3 years at 8 per cent = PV of £1 for 2 years at 8 per cent × PV of £1 for 1 year at 8 per cent

= 0.8574 × 0.926

= 0.7939

Example. Given that the Amount of £1 per annum in 45 years at $1\frac{1}{4}$ per cent is 60, calculate the PV of £1 in 45 years at $1\frac{1}{4}$ per cent.

$$\text{Amount of £1 per annum} = \frac{A - 1}{i}$$

$$\text{PV of £1} = \frac{1}{A}$$

So that the common factor is A

$$60 = \frac{A - 1}{0.0125}$$

$$(60 \times 0.0125) + 1 = A$$

$$1.75 = A$$

But PV = $1/A$, so that

PV of £1 for 45 years at $1\frac{1}{4}$ per cent

$$= \frac{1}{1.75} = 0.5715$$

Example. Calculate the YP for 16 years at 10 per cent and 3 per cent, given that the YP Single Rate at 3 per cent for 16 years is 12.561.

$$\text{YP Single Rate} = \frac{1 - PV}{i} \quad \text{But} \quad \frac{PV}{A} = \frac{1}{A}$$

$$\text{YP Dual Rate} = \frac{1}{i + s} \quad \text{But} \quad s = \frac{i}{A - 1}$$

The method is to derive A from the first formula, and substitute this in s, which is to be used in the second formula.

$$12.561 = \frac{1 - PV}{0.03}$$

$$(12.561 \times 0.03) = 1 - PV$$
$$PV = 1 - (12.561 \times 0.03)$$
$$= 1 - 0.37683$$
$$= 0.62317$$

So that

$$A \text{ for 16 years at 3 per cent} = \frac{1}{0.62317}$$

$$= 1.605$$

$s = i/(A - 1)$ for 16 years at 3 per cent

$$s = \frac{0.03}{1.605 - 1}$$

$$= \frac{0.03}{0.605} = 0.049$$

Substituting in the YP formula $1/(i + s)$

YP for 16 years at 10 per cent and 3 per cent

$$= \frac{1}{0.10 + 0.049}$$

$$= \frac{1}{0.149}$$

$$= 6.711$$

Example. Value an income of £1000 per annum for 10 years at 10 per cent and $2\frac{1}{2}$ per cent net adjusted for tax at 40p in £, given that the Annual Sinking fund to replace £1 in 10 years at $2\frac{1}{2}$ per cent is 0.08925.

s for 10 years at $2\frac{1}{2}$ per cent = 0.08925

Net income per annum   = £1000

YP for 10 years at 10 per cent and $2\frac{1}{2}$ per cent (tax 40p in £)

$$= \cfrac{1}{i + s\left(\cfrac{1}{1 - x}\right)} = \cfrac{1}{0.10 + \left(0.08925 \times \cfrac{1}{0.6}\right)}$$

$$= \cfrac{1}{0.10 + 0.1487}$$

$$= \cfrac{1}{0.2487} = 4.02$$

Capital value = £4020

Another type of question may involve the use of algebraic expressions.

Example. If the Amount of £1 in *n* years at 10 per cent is *p*, express the Present Value of £1 in *n* + 1 years at 10 per cent in terms of *p*.

A for *n* years at 10 per cent = $(1 + i)^n = p$

So that

A for 1 year at 10 per cent = $\sqrt[n]{p}$

PV for 1 year at 10 per cent = $\cfrac{1}{\sqrt[n]{p}}$

Thus

PV for (*n* + 1) years at 10 per cent = $\cfrac{1}{\left(\sqrt[n]{p}\right)^{n + 1}}$

Questions may be asked to test a candidate's knowledge of Dual Rate principles and the effect of tax on the sinking fund element and the sinking fund interest.

Example. Your client, Mr Mutt, recently bought at auction an interest in a property yielding £100 per annum net. He paid £1000 for this interest which gives him, he says, a clear 10 per cent return. You happen to know that the interest has only 18 years' unexpired term. Calculate for Mr Mutt his true return, correct to two places of decimals, after allowing for a sinking fund at 3 per cent throughout (no allowance for tax).

Perpetual interest = 10 per cent

So that

$$YP = \frac{1}{i} = \frac{1}{0.10} = 10$$

But income is for 18 years only; thus

$$YP \text{ of } 10 = \frac{1}{i + s}$$

$$10 = \frac{1}{i + \dfrac{0.03}{1.03^{18} - 1}}$$

$$10 = \frac{1}{i + 0.0428}$$

$$10(i + 0.0428) = 1$$

$$i = \frac{1 - 0.428}{10}$$

$$= \frac{0.572}{10} = 0.0572$$

$$= 5.72 \text{ per cent}$$

Example. An investor has purchased a leasehold interest in a shop for £6000. The lease has an unexpired term of 15 years and yields a net income of £1000 per annum. Assuming that a sinking fund can be invested at 3 per cent net calculate

  (i) the yield of the investment ignoring the effect of tax on the sinking fund element of the income, and
  (ii) effective yield after allowing for tax at 40p in £.

Capital value = Net income per annum × YP

$$£6000 = £1000 \times YP$$

So that

$$YP = 6$$

(i) YP for 15 years at i and 3 per cent is

$$6 = \frac{1}{i + s}$$

$$= \frac{1}{i + \dfrac{0.03}{1.03^{15} - 1}}$$

$$6 = \frac{1}{i + 0.0538}$$

$$6(i + 0.0538) = 1$$

$$i = \frac{1 - (6 \times 0.0538)}{6}$$

$$= \frac{1 - 0.3228}{6}$$

$$= \frac{0.6722}{6} = 0.1128$$

$$= 11.28 \text{ per cent}$$

(ii) YP for 15 years at i and 3 per cent net (tax 40p in £) is

$$6 = \frac{1}{i + s\left(\dfrac{1}{1 - x}\right)}$$

$$6 = \frac{1}{i + \left(0.0538 \times \dfrac{1}{0.6}\right)}$$

$$6 = \frac{1}{i + 0.0897}$$

$$6(i + 0.0897) = 1$$

$$i = \frac{1 - (6 \times 0.00897)}{6}$$

$$= \frac{1 - 0.5382}{6}$$

$$= \frac{0.4618}{6} = 0.077$$

$$= 7.7 \text{ per cent}$$

The following questions are from the examinations of universities and professional bodies and should be used for practice and revision purposes. They should be calculated without the use of valuation tables.

QUESTIONS

5.14 Given that the Amount of £1 per annum in 10 years at 10 per cent = 15.937 and that $(1.10)^9$ = 2.358, calculate the PV of £1 for 19 years at 10 per cent.

5.15 Given that the Years' Purchase of a reversion to a perpetuity at 10 per cent after 19 years is 1.635, calculate the Annual Sinking fund to produce £1 in 20 years at 10 per cent.

5.16 Given that the YP in perpetuity at 10 per cent deferred 24 years is 1.0, calculate the Amount of £1 per annum for 24 years at 10 per cent.

5.17 Given that the Amount of £1 per annum in 6 years at 7 per cent = 7.153 and that $(1.07)^5$ = 1.403, calculate the PV of £1 for 11 years at 7 per cent.

5.18 Calculate the Annual Sinking fund to replace £1 in 15 years at 6 per cent, given that the PV of £1 in 15 years at 6 per cent = 0.4173.

5.19 Given that the PV of £1 in 47 years at 5 per cent = 0.1, calculate (i) the Annual Sinking fund to produce £1 in 47 years at 5 per cent; (ii) the Present Value of £1 per annum in 47 years at 5 per cent. (The result of (i) must not be used to find (ii).)

5.20 Given that the Amount of £1 per annum in 10 years at 4 per cent = 12, calculate the Years' Purchase for 10 years at 8 per cent and 4 per cent net, adjusted for tax at 50 per cent.

5.21 Calculate the Annual Sinking fund in 30 years at $5\frac{1}{2}$ per cent, given that the PV of £1 in 30 years at $5\frac{1}{2}$ per cent is 0.20.

5.22 Calculate the Present Value of £1 per annum in 11 years at 7 per cent, given that the PV of £1 in 11 years at 7 per cent is 0.475.

5.23 Calculate the Amount of £1 per annum in 20 years at $7\frac{3}{4}$ per cent, given that the Years' Purchase in 20 years at $7\frac{3}{4}$ per cent is 10.0.

5.24 The Present Value of £y in 8 years at 10 per cent = x. What is the Amount of £1 per annum in 8 years at 10 per cent in terms of x and y?

5.25 Explain what the figure of £330 represents in the following calculation

£100 p.a.

Amount of £1 per annum for 6 years at 6 per cent	= 7
× PV of £1 in 6 years at 6 per cent	= 0.7
	4.9
× PV of £1 in 7 years at 6 per cent	= 0.67

3.3
£330

5.26 Identify the following resultant figure of 3.337 and show another method of obtaining the same result

Present Value of £1 in 5 years at 6 per cent = 0.7473
Present Value of £1 in 6 years at 6 per cent = 0.7049
Present Value of £1 in 7 years at 6 per cent = 0.6651
Present Value of £1 in 8 years at 6 per cent = 0.6274
Present Value of £1 in 9 years at 6 per cent = 0.5919
3.3366

3.337

5.27 A purchaser walked into an auction room and bid 10 YP for a stream of income, believing it to be perpetual. He later discovered that the income only lasts for 25 years. Allowing for a sinking fund for redemption of capital at 4 per cent gross and tax at 25p in £, what will be the real rate of interest he will enjoy?

5.28 Using a 10 per cent basis, what is the result of investing £1 at the end of each year for a period of 10 years, followed by £2 at the end of each year for the following 10 years?

5.29 £1000 has to be replaced by means of an annual sinking fund over a total period of 10 years. Using a rate of $2\frac{1}{2}$ per cent net and allowing for the fact that the sinking fund in the last five years is to be twice that during the first 5 years what is the annual premium during the first period?

5.30 If, after investing a certain sum of money annually at the end of each of 5 years, and thereafter twice that sum annually at the end of each of the next 5 years, you had accumulated £22 630, what were the annual instalments in each of the 5 year periods respectively, allowing for compound interest throughout the 10 years at 5 per cent?

5.31 Given that the Amount of £1 in 9 years at 8 per cent = £2, calculate the monthly instalment (comprising interest and capital repayment) required to redeem a mortgage loan of £5000 over a period of 10 years at 8 per cent.

5.32 Calculate the capital outstanding on a mortgage of £3000 granted 9 years ago for a period of 10 years at 6 per cent per annum, given that the annual sinking fund to replace £1 in 10 years at 6 per cent is 0.07587.

5.33 (i) Calculate the capital value of the right to receive a fixed profit rent of £2000 per annum for 5 years, assuming a remunerative return of 10 per cent per annum and an accumulative rate of 3 per cent per annum.

(ii) Show that a remunerative return of 10 per cent is achieved, and the original capital value is recouped after 5 years.

5.34 An income of £2000 per annum receivable in arrears and lasting for 5 years capitalized at 10 per cent single rate gives

Income per annum = £2000
YP for 5 years at 10
          per cent = 3.79
Capital value = £7580

(i) Show that the capital value, if invested at 10 per cent, will produce an income of £2000 per annum in arrears for 5 years.
(ii) What is the annual return required from the income in order to give 10 per cent on outlay?
(iii) What is the purpose of the balance between the 10 per cent return on outlay and the £2000 per annum income?

5.6 ADJUSTMENT OF FORMULAE FOR INCOMES OTHER THAN ANNUALLY IN ARREARS

The formulae derived earlier assume that income is received annually at the end of years, and Parry's *Valuation and Investment Tables* are based upon this assumption.

It is likely that, where property is let, rents will be received in advance, probably on a quarterly basis, and both P. Bowcock and J.J. Rose allow for this in their tables.

The Years' Purchase in perpetuity, shown earlier as $\frac{1}{i}$ may be adjusted by using the following formulae and obtaining the following results.

Assuming a yield of 8 per cent

	Formulae	YP
YP in perpetuity – income annually in advance	$\dfrac{1 + i}{i}$	13.5
YP in perpetuity – income quarterly in advance	$\dfrac{1}{4\left(1 - \sqrt[4]{\dfrac{1}{1 + i}}\right)}$	13.119
YP in perpetuity – income quarterly in arrear	$\dfrac{1}{4(\sqrt[4]{1 + i}) - 1)}$	12. 869

If Years' Purchase single rate with income quarterly in advance is required this may be obtained from the formula

$$YP = \dfrac{\dfrac{1}{4}\left(1 - \dfrac{1}{(1 + i)^n}\right)}{1 - \sqrt[4]{\dfrac{1}{1 + i}}}$$

Example. Calculate the Years' Purchase for 8 years at 8 per cent assuming income quarterly in advance.

$$YP = \dfrac{\dfrac{1}{4}\left(1 - \dfrac{1}{1.08^8}\right)}{1 - \sqrt[4]{\dfrac{1}{1.08}}}$$

$$= \dfrac{\dfrac{1}{4}(1 - 0.5403)}{1 - 0.98094} = 6.03$$

It may not only be Years' Purchase tables which need adjustments for quarterly in advance payments. Sinking fund payments may be required quarterly in advance.

The formula for 's' annually in arrears has been proved as $\dfrac{i}{(1 + i)^n - 1}$

For quarterly in advance, the total annual allowance, $s =$

$$\frac{4 \times \left(1 - \sqrt[4]{\dfrac{1}{1 + i}}\right)}{((1 + i)^n - 1)}$$

Example. Calculate the annual sinking fund to produce £1 in 8 years at 3 per cent, payments quarterly in advance.

$$s = \frac{4 \times 1 - \sqrt[4]{\dfrac{1}{1.03}}}{1.03^8 - 1}$$

$$= \frac{4 \times 1 - 0.9926}{0.2668} = 0.1109$$

This sinking fund adjustment will be used if the Years' Purchase dual rate with income receivable quarterly in advance and sinking fund payable quarterly in advance is required.

The YP dual rate with tax has been shown as $\dfrac{1}{i + \left[s\ \text{net}\left(\dfrac{1}{1 - x}\right)\right]}$

This may be adjusted to

$$YP = \frac{1}{4\left[1 - \sqrt[4]{\dfrac{1}{1 + i}}\right] + 4\left[\dfrac{1 - \sqrt[4]{\dfrac{1}{1 + i}} \times \dfrac{1}{1 - x}}{(1 + i)^n - 1}\right]}$$

Example. Calculate Years' Purchase for 8 years at 8 per cent and 3 per cent net tax 30p in £, both income and sinking fund quarterly in advance.

$$YP = \cfrac{1}{4\left[1 - \sqrt[4]{\cfrac{1}{1.08}}\right] + \left(0.1109 \times \cfrac{1}{0.7}\right)}$$

$$= \cfrac{1}{(4 \times 0.0191) + 0.1584} \qquad = 4.259$$

6 Discounted Cash Flow Techniques

6.1 NET PRESENT VALUE (NPV)

The calculation of Net Present Value (NPV) requires the discounting of all future income and expenditure in an investment situation at a rate of interest, which may be termed a 'target rate'. The NPV is the surplus or deficit which accrues when the immediate and discounted future expenditure is set against the discounted future income. The discounting is achieved by the use of the Present Value of £1 table, explained in Chapter 5.

Example. Find the Net Present Value of the following 4 years cash flow using a target rate of 8 per cent.

	End of year 1	2	3	4
Outflow	£14 500			
Inflow		£5000	£6000	£7000

		Discounted Outflow	*Discounted Inflow*
	1	−£14 500 × 0.926 = £13 427	
	2		+ £5000 × 0.857 = + £4285
	3		+ £6000 × 0.794 = + £4764
	4		+ £7000 × 0.735 = + £5145
	Totals	−£13 427	+ £14 194

$$\text{NPV} = £14\,194 - £13\,427 = +£767$$

The discount figures in the above are the appropriate Present Values of £1 at 8 per cent.

It can be seen that the NPV is a surplus of £767 when a target rate of 8 per cent is used; this is a profit over and above an 8 per cent return on capital and the return of the outlay.

99

Assume that the same cash flow is now to be discounted at a target rate of 12 per cent.

		Discounted Outflow	Discounted Inflow
End of year	1	$-£14\,500 \times 0.893 = -£12\,948$	
	2		$+ £5000 \times 0.797 = +£3985$
	3		$+ £6000 \times 0.712 = +£4272$
	4		$+ £7000 \times 0.636 = +£4452$
	Totals	$- £12\,948$	$+£12\,709$

$$\text{NPV} = \quad -£12\,948 + £12\,709 = -£239$$

By the use of the higher target rate, a surplus of £767 has changed into a deficit of £239. A general rule can be stated – the higher the target rate of interest, the lower the NPV.

The calculation of Net Present Values may be used to compare different cash flow situations and to see which gives the highest NPV.

6.2 INTERNAL RATE OF RETURN (IRR)

The disadvantage of calculating NPVs to compare different cash flows is that so much depends on the choice of the target rate. The scheme giving the best NPV at a certain target rate may not be the best if the rate is altered. It is better to compare cash flows by calculating the Internal Rate of Return (IRR). This is the discount rate at which the discounted income equates with initial and discounted outlay: i.e. the rate at which the NPV = 0.

If cash flows are compared on this basis, the best situation will be the one with the highest IRR.

In the previous example, at a rate of 8 per cent the NPV is + £767 and at 12 per cent the NPV is −£239. The IRR must lie between 8 and 12 per cent and may be found by similar triangles.

Let the base line of the triangle = difference between the two target rates i.e. $12 - 8 = 4$; the height of the triangle = total value of NPVs (ignoring signs); x = IRR - lower rate of interest.

Then $\dfrac{x}{767} = \dfrac{4}{1006}$

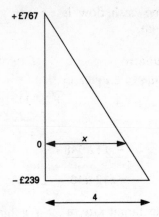

$$x = \frac{4 \times 767}{1006} = 3.05$$

IRR = 8 + 3.05 = say 11 per cent

The result is slightly inaccurate, because the hypotenuse of the triangle is slightly curved.

An inaccuracy can be reduced by having two target rates which are fairly close together: for example, in the above, 10 and 12 per cent.

Example. A freehold shop investment is being offered for sale for £175 000. It has a net income of £10 000 per annum receivable for 3 years. The current net rack rental value is considered to be £15 000 per annum.

Calculate the Internal Rate of Return.

Assume a target rate of 7 per cent, and calculate the net present value.

There is an income flow of £10 000 per annum for each of 3 years; as shown in Chapter 5, the £10 000 per annum can be multiplied by the YP for 3 years at 7 per cent to give its capital value. In 3 years' time, the income will revert to £15 000 per annum; this can be multiplied by the YP in perpetuity at 7 per cent deferred 3 years.

Net income per annum   = £10 000

YP for 3 years at 7 per cent   =   2.624

                                                                        £26 240

Reversion

Net rack rental value per annum   = £15 000

YP in perpetuity deferred 3
years at 7 per cent   = 11.661

                                                                        £174 915

                        Capital value   = £201 155

                        Less Initial outlay   = £175 000

                        Net Present Value   = +£26 155

The target rate of 7 per cent gives a Net Present Value of + £26 155; recalculate the valuation using a target rate of say 10 per cent.

Net income per annum   = £10 000

YP for 3 years at 10 per cent   =   2.487

                                                                        £24 870

Reversion

Net rack rental value per annum   = £15 000

YP in perpetuity deferred 3
years at 10 per cent   =   7.513

                                                                        £112 695

                        Capital value   = £137 565

                        Less Initial outlay   = £175 000

                        Net Present Value   = −£37 435

The IRR must lie between 7 per cent and 10 per cent, and may be found by similar triangles.
Let the base line of the triangle = difference between the two target rates, ie 10 − 7 = 3; the height of the triangle = total value of NPVs (ignoring signs); x = IRR − lower rate of interest.

Then $\dfrac{x}{26\,155} = \dfrac{3}{63\,590}$

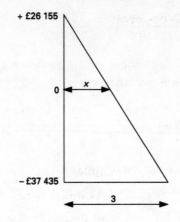

$$x = \frac{3 \times 26\,155}{63\,590} = 1.234$$

$$IRR = 7 + 1.234 = (\text{say}) \; 8\tfrac{1}{4} \text{ per cent.}$$

6.2.1   Internal Rate of Return Tables

Parry's Valuation and Investment Tables provide Internal Rate of Return tables:

(i)   without reflecting rental growth.

It is, however, necessary to carry out some preliminary calculations.

Example. The freehold interest in a property has recently been purchased for £259 500. The property is let on lease having 3 years unexpired at a net rent of £10 000 per annum. The net rack rental value is £20 000 per annum.
Calculate the Internal Rate of Return.

Preliminary Calculations

$$Initial \; Yield \; = \frac{\text{net income}}{\text{price}} \times 100 \text{ per cent}$$

$$= \frac{10\,000}{259\,500} \times 100 = 3.85$$

Rental factor = $\dfrac{\text{full rental value}}{\text{net income}}$ = $\dfrac{20\,000}{10\,000}$ = 2

From the tables, an initial yield of $3\frac{1}{2}$ per cent gives 6.41, 4 per cent gives 7.24.

By interpolation,
an initial yield of 3.85 gives

$$\left(\frac{0.35}{0.5} \times \text{difference in IRR}\right) + 6.41$$

$$= \left(\frac{0.35}{0.5} \times 0.83\right) + 6.41$$

= 6.99 (say) 7 per cent.

(ii) reflecting rental growth.

Taking the previous example, assuming a rental growth of 7 per cent per annum, the preliminary calculations are the same. From the tables, an initial yield of $3\frac{1}{2}$ per cent gives 7.58, 4 per cent gives 8.54.

By interpolation, an initial yield of 3.85 gives

$$\left(\frac{0.35}{0.5} \times 0.96\right) + 7.58$$

= 8.252 (say) 8¼ per cent.

QUESTIONS

6.1 A cash flow has the following outflow/inflow pattern.

	Immediate	End of year 1	2	3	4
Outflow	£36 000				
Inflow		£10 000	£11 000	£12 000	£13 000

Calculate the Net Present Value if the target rate is 9 per cent, and the Internal Rate of Return.

6.2 A freehold shop investment is being offered for sale for £213 500.

It has a net income of £15 000 per annum receivable for 2 years. The current net rack rental value is considered to be £20 000 per annum.

Calculate the Internal Rate of Return.

6.3 A freehold investment is being offered for sale for £322 500. It is anticipated that net rental per annum will be obtainable for the next 30 years with a commencing rent of £20 000 per annum, subject to 5 year rent reviews.

It is considered that, at each rent review, the rent will increase by 5 per cent per annum, and that the value of the residue in 30 years' time will be £200 000.

Calculate the Internal Rate of Return.

7 The Valuation of Freehold and Leasehold Interests

It has been shown in Chapters 3 and 5 that one method of obtaining the capital value of an interest in property is the Investment Method, namely

Capital value = Net income per annum × Years' Purchase

Net income may be derived from the rent received per annum less outgoings. Years' Purchase will differ according to the yield an investor expects from the property investment; it is suggested that the reader uses the pattern of yields included in Chapter 3 as a guide when carrying out valuation exercises.

Once the term of years and yield have been determined, reference can be made to the appropriate table in Parry's *Valuation and Investment Tables*.

In this chapter, calculations of capital value will be assessed to the nearest £50.

7.1 FREEHOLD INTERESTS

The tables normally used for the valuation of freehold interests are

(1) Years' Purchase Single Rate
(2) Present Value of £1
(3) Years' Purchase of a Reversion to a Perpetuity

The method may differ according to whether the net income is perpetual, variable or deferred.

7.1.1 Perpetual Income

Property may be let on full repairing and insuring terms at a rent which is equivalent to rack rental value, the lease having no provisions for regular rent reviews. In these circumstances, it may be assumed that the rent will be receivable in perpetuity.

Example. A freehold shop in a provincial town centre has recently been let on full repairing and insuring terms at a rack rent of £5000 per annum. Value the freehold interest.

Assuming a freehold yield on rack rental value terms of 7 per cent

Net income per annum	=	£5000
YP in perpetuity at 7 per cent	=	14.286
Capital value	=	£71 430
(say)		£71 500

A lease may provide for regular rent reviews, the rent revision to be calculated at the time of the review. This amount cannot be predetermined when valuing the freehold interest, and so the rent reviews are recognised by adjusting the yield.

Example. Modern freehold office premises are let on internal repairing terms at a rent of £5000 per annum. The lease provides for rent reviews at 5-yearly intervals. Value the freehold interest.

Assuming a freehold yield on rack rental value terms of 8 per cent

Rent received per annum			£5000
Less			
External repairs and insurance say 15 per cent of rack rent	= £750		
Management say 5 per cent of rack rent	= £250	£1000	
Net income per annum		£4000	
YP in perpetuity at 8 per cent	=	12.5	
Capital value	=	£50 000	

7.1.2 Varying and Deferred Incomes

In many freehold interests, the annual income will vary because an existing lease will expire after a known period. The rent being paid may not be the current rack rental value, because it was agreed at some date in the past, and since then values have increased.

Example. A freehold shop in a good trading position is let on full repairing and insuring terms at a rent of £5000 per annum, the lease having 5 years unexpired. The current net rack rental value is £10 000 per annum. Value the freehold interest.

There are two different rents to be capitalised, namely (i) £5000 per annum receivable for 5 years only (the unexpired period of the lease) and (ii) £10 000 per annum receivable in perpetuity, but deferred 5 years (the reversion). It may be considered that the £5000 per annum is secure income, because the tenant is paying a rent, which is half of the full rental value. (The £5000 per annum is said to be *twice secured.*) Hence, the tenant will attempt to comply with all the terms of the lease, so that he does not jeopardise his occupation and the considerable profit rent which he enjoys. Because of the security, the freehold yield on rack rental terms adopted for the reversion may be reduced by, say, 1 per cent for the unexpired period.

It should be emphasised, however, that the position may be different in the case of a long unexpired term and a fixed income. The benefit of security will be cancelled out by the disadvantage of receiving fixed income over a long period, with no protection against inflation.

The appropriate calculation follows, assuming a freehold yield on rack rental value terms to be 7 per cent.

Unexpired term of lease is 5 years

Rent received per annum	= £5000
YP for 5 years at 6 per cent	= 4.212
	£21 060

Reversion

Net rack rental value per annum	= £10 000

YP in perpetuity at 7 per cent
deferred 5 years   = 10.186
                                                         —————

                                                         £101 860
                                                         ————————
                            Capital value   = £122 920
                                                         ————————
                            (say)   £122 900

(*Note* The figure of 10.186 is obtained from the Years' Purchase of a Reversion to a Perpetuity table.)

A second reason for variations in annual income is that the lease may incorporate rent reviews, with the amount to be paid at each review period agreed at the commencement of the lease.

Example. Freehold office premises were let 4 years ago on a full repairing and insuring lease for a period of 14 years. It was agreed that the rent for the first 7 years would be £5000 per annum, and for the second 7 years, £6000 per annum. The current net rack rental value is £7000 per annum. Value the freehold interest.

This valuation has three different rents to be capitalised, namely

    (i) £5000 per annum receivable for 3 years only,
    (ii) £6000 per annum receivable for 7 years only but deferred 3 years, and
    (iii) £7000 per annum receivable in perpetuity, but deferred 10 years.

As in the previous example, the rents received under the lease may be considered to be slightly more secure than the rack rental value, and the yield adjusted accordingly.

The capital value of the £6000 per annum may be obtained by multiplying the rent per annum by a deferred Years' Purchase. This is obtained by multiplying together the YP for the period of receipt (7 years) and the PV of £1 for the period of deferment (3 years).

The appropriate calculation follows assuming a freehold yield on rack rental value terms to be 7 per cent.

Unexpired term of lease is 3 years

Rent received per annum   = £5000

YP for 3 years at 6 per cent   = 2.673
                                                         —————

                                                         £13 365

7 years

Rent received per annum		= £6000
YP for 7 years at 6 per cent	= 5.582	
PV of £1 in 3 years at 6 per cent	= <u>0.84</u>	
YP for 7 years at 6 per cent deferred 3 years	= <u>4.689</u>	
		£28 134

Reversion

Net rack rental value per annum		= £7000
YP in perpetuity at 7 per cent deferred 10 years	= <u>7.262</u>	<u>£50 834</u>
Capital value		= <u>£92 333</u>
(say)		£92 350

The deferment of Years' Purchase may be undertaken by either of two methods.

(i) By multiplying together the YP for the period of receipt and the PV of £1 for the period of deferment (as illustrated in the previous example); or

(ii) Deduct the YP for the period of deferment from the YP for the period from the time of valuation to the time of expiration of the income. The two methods may be illustrated by an example.

Example. £1000 per annum is to be received from a letting of freehold agricultural land for a period of 15 years commencing in 10 years' time. What is the capital value of this annual income?

Assuming a freehold yield on rack rental value terms to be 5 per cent and using (i)

Rent received per annum		= £1000
YP for 15 years at 5 per cent	= 10.380	
PV of £1 in 10 years at 5 per cent	= <u>0.614</u>	

YP for 15 years at 5 per cent deferred 10 years		= 6.373
	Capital value	= £6373
	(say)	£6350

using (ii)

Rent received per annum		= £1000
YP for 25 years at 5 per cent	= 14.094	
Less YP for 10 years at 5 per cent	= 7.722	
YP for 15 years at 5 per cent deferred 10 years		= 6.372
	Capital value	= £6372
	(say)	£6350

The first method is usually adopted, because it may also be applied to Dual Rate situations (see later in this chapter).

There may be instances where the unexpired period of a lease is very long. In these cases, it may be more practical to treat the income as perpetual, if it is fixed throughout the period of the lease.

Example. Land has been let at a ground rent of £500 per annum, the ground lease having 50 years unexpired. Factory premises have been built on the site, having a current net rack rental value of £2000 per annum. Value the freehold interest, assuming that the freehold yield for a ground rent with a long unexpired term and fixed income is 15 per cent, and for factory premises let on rack rental value terms (but long wait for reversion) is 12 per cent.

Ground lease is 50 years

Rent received per annum	= £500	
YP for 50 years at 15 per cent	= 6.6605	
		£3330

Reversion

Net rack rental value per annum	= £2000	
YP in perpetuity at 12 per cent deferred 50 years	= 0.029	
		£ 58

Capital Value	£3388
(say)	£3400

Alternatively, the ground rent may be treated as being perpetual and the reversionary income ignored.

Rent received per annum	= £500
YP in perpetuity at 15 per cent	= 6.667
Capital value	= £3333
(say)	£3350

The calculations for freehold valuations involving terms and reversions have been based to date on the assumption that the income for the term is very secure. The yield has been shown as 1 per cent less than that used for reversion. This *traditional approach* has been extensively used in freehold valuations.

However, with the decimation of income's purchasing power, it is reasonable to assume that the income receivable under the term of a lease is very *inflation-prone* and has no opportunity for growth. To counteract this, it may be appropriate to apply a yield 2 or 3 per cent above the yield for *gilts* say 15 per cent.

Taking a situation used earlier in this chapter:

Example: A freehold shop in a good trading position is let on full repairing and insuring terms at a rent of £5000 per annum, the lease having 5 years unexpired. The current net rack rental value is £10 000 per annum. Value the freehold interest.

The appropriate calculation follows, assuming a freehold yield on rack rental value terms to be 7 per cent, and the yield for the term to be 15 per cent.

Unexpired term of lease is 5 years

Rent received per annum	= £5000	
YP for 5 years at 15 per cent	= 3.352	
		= £16 760

Reversion

Net rack rental value per annum	= £10 000
YP in perpetuity deferred 5	

years at 7 per cent   = <u>10.186</u>

                                             = <u>£101 860</u>

            Capital value   = <u>£118 620</u>

            (say)   = <u>£118 650</u>

This gives a capital value of £118 650, compared with £122 900, when a yield of 6 per cent for the 5 year term was used.

The higher yield for term income will be adopted in later examples of valuations of freehold interests.

7.1.3 Hardcore or Layer Method

The conventional valuation with a traditional yield is as follows:

Example. A property is let on full repairing and insuring terms with 4 years unexpired at a rent of £10 000 per annum. The current net rack rental value is £15 000 per annum.

Similar properties show a yield of 6 per cent.

Conventional Valuation

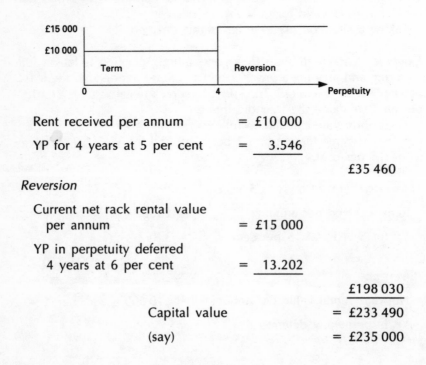

Rent received per annum   = £10 000

YP for 4 years at 5 per cent   = <u> 3.546</u>

                                                £35 460

Reversion

Current net rack rental value
    per annum   = £15 000

YP in perpetuity deferred
    4 years at 6 per cent   = <u> 13.202</u>

                                               £198 030

            Capital value   = £233 490

            (say)   = £235 000

The flow of income in the above calculation has been *vertically sliced*.

Hardcore or Layer Method

This method adopts a valuation where the income flow is *horizontally sliced*.

Taking the previous example,

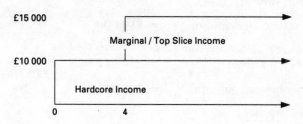

Hardcore income per annum	= £10 000	
YP in perpetuity at 5 per cent	= 20	
		£200 000
Marginal income per annum	= £5000	
YP in perpetuity deferred 4 years at 6 per cent	= 13.202	
		£ 66 010
		£266 010
(say)		£265 000

This calculation has assumed that the marginal income (the difference between current net rack rental value and the term rent) is slightly riskier than term rent and is capitalised at 1 per cent higher. To obtain a more accurate yield for the marginal income, preliminary calculations may be prepared as follows:

Preliminary Calculations

Current net rack rental value per annum	= £15 000	
YP in perpetuity at 6 per cent	= 16.667	
		£250 000
Less Rent received per annum	= £10 000	

YP in perpetuity at 5 per cent   =   <u>20</u>

£200 000

Capital value of marginal income   <u>£ 50 000</u>

Yield on marginal income

$$\frac{5000}{50\,000} \times 100 = 10 \text{ per cent}$$

The valuation then becomes:

Hardcore income per annum   = £10 000

YP in perpetuity at 5 per cent   =   <u>20</u>

£200 000

Marginal income per annum   = £5000

YP in perpetuity deferred 4
years at 10 per cent   =   <u>6.83</u>

£ 34 150

Capital Value   = <u>£234 150</u>

(say)   = £235 000

For a more detailed consideration of this method, reference may be made to Diane Butler, *Applied Valuation* (Macmillan 1987) and David Isaac and Terry Steley, *Property Valuation Techniques* (Macmillan 1991).

7.2 LEASEHOLD INTERESTS

The tables normally used for the valuation of leasehold interests are

   (i) Years' Purchase Dual Rate adjusted for tax (throughout the calculations a tax rate of 30p in £ will be used); and
   (ii) Present Value of £1.

The valuation may differ according to whether or not the net income or profit rent at the time of valuation is fixed throughout the term of the lease, or is variable, or is deferred.

   If the property is sublet by the lessee then net income is capitalised; if the lessee occupies the property, then profit rent is capitalised.

7.2.1 Fixed Income for the Period of the Lease

If premises are let on lease at a fixed rent throughout the period of the lease, and the lessee sublets also at a fixed rent, then net income will be constant throughout the lease.

Example. A shop was let on a full repairing and insuring lease at a rent of £10 000 per annum, the lease having 8 years unexpired. The premises have been sublet on the same terms at a rent of £12 500 per annum, the sublease expiring 3 days before the main lease. The current net rack rental value is £16 000 per annum. Value the leasehold and subleasehold interests.

Assuming a freehold yield on rack rental value terms to be 7 per cent, then a leasehold interest involves greater risk and an appropriate yield would be 8 per cent. The subleasehold may be $8\frac{1}{2}$ per cent. Tax liability is 30p in £.

Leasehold Interest

Rent received per annum	= £12 500
Less Rent paid per annum	= £10 000
Net income per annum	= £ 2 500
YP for 8 years at 8 per cent and $2\frac{1}{2}$ per cent net (tax 30p in £)	= 4.106
Capital value	= £10 265
(say)	£10 250

Subleasehold Interest

Net rack rental value per annum	= £16 000
Less Rent paid per annum	= £12 500
Profit rent per annum	= £ 3 500
YP for 8 years at $8\frac{1}{2}$ per cent and $2\frac{1}{2}$ per cent net (tax 30p in £)	= 4.024
Capital value	= £14 084
(say)	£14 100

7.2.2 Varying and Deferred Incomes during the Period of the Lease

The net income to be capitalised may vary for two reasons

(i) The rent to be paid to the freeholder or lessor may be regularly reviewed during the period of the lease, and/or

(ii) the rent received from a sublessee may be reviewed during the sublease period.

In the case of an occupying lessee or sublessee, the profit rent may vary because of rent reviews.

Example. Office premises have been let by the freeholder on a full repairing and insuring lease, the lease having 14 years unexpired; the rent to be paid for the next 7 years is £10 000 per annum and for the 7 years thereafter is £12 500 per annum. The premises have been sublet, the sublease expiring 3 days before the main lease; the rent to be paid for the next 7 years is £13 500 per annum and for the 7 years thereafter is £15 500 per annum. The current net rack rental value is £17 500 per annum. Value the leasehold and subleasehold interests.

Leasehold interest This valuation has two different net incomes, namely

(i) £3500 per annum (£13 500 – £10 000) receivable for 7 years and

(ii) £3000 per annum (£15 500 – £12 500) receivable for 7 years, but deferred 7 years.

The £3000 per annum is capitalised by a deferred YP. This is obtained by multiplying together the YP for the period of receipt and the PV of £1 for the period of deferment. Thus, assuming a leasehold yield to be 7 per cent (1 per cent more than freehold yield on rack rental value terms), and a tax liability of 30p in £

First 7 Years

Rent received per annum	= £13 500
Less Rent paid per annum	= £10 000
Net income per annum	= £ 3 500

YP for 7 years at 7 per annum and $2\frac{1}{2}$

per cent net (tax 30p in £)   = 3.857

                                                                  £13 500

Second 7 Years

Rent received per annum   = £15 500

Less Rent paid per annum   = £12 500

Net income per annum   = £ 3 000

YP for 7 years at 7 per cent and $2\frac{1}{2}$
per cent net (tax 30p in £)   = 3.857

PV of £1 in 7 years at 7
per cent   = 0.623

YP for 7 years at 7 per cent and
$2\frac{1}{2}$ per cent (tax 30p in £)
deferred 7 years   = 2.403

                                                                  £ 7 209

                   Capital value   = £20 709

                   (say)   £20 700

Subleasehold interest This valuation has two differing amounts of profit rent, namely

   (i) £4000 per annum (£17 500 − £13 500) receivable for 7 years and
   (ii) £2000 per annum (£17 500 − £15 500) receivable for 7 years, but deferred 7 years.

Assuming a subleasehold yield of $7\frac{1}{2}$ per cent ($\frac{1}{2}$ per cent more than leasehold) and a tax liability of 30p in £

First 7 Years

Net rack rental value per annum   = £17 500

Less Rent paid per annum   = £13 500

                   Profit rent per annum   = £ 4 000

YP for 7 years at $7\frac{1}{2}$ per cent and $2\frac{1}{2}$
per cent net (tax 30p in £)   = 3.784

                                                                  £15 136

Second 7 Years

Net rack rental value per annum	=	£17 500
Less Rent paid per annum	=	£15 500
Profit rent per annum	=	£ 2 000

YP for 7 years at $7\frac{1}{2}$ per
cent and $2\frac{1}{2}$ per cent net
(tax 30p in £)   = 3.784

PV of £1 in 7 years at
$7\frac{1}{2}$ per cent   = 0.603

YP for 7 years at $7\frac{1}{2}$ per cent and
$2\frac{1}{2}$ per cent net (tax 30p in £)
deferred 7 years   = 2.282

$$\frac{£\ \ 4\ 564}{}$$

Capital value   = £19 700

7.2.3 Non-tax-paying Investors

Some investors such as charities have complete or partial exemption from tax-paying commitments. These investors will be attracted by short-term leasehold interests, because they will not have to take tax into account when setting aside a sinking fund to recoup the capital used to purchase the property.

Example. A property, let on a full repairing and insuring lease having 10 years unexpired, provides a net income of £1000 per annum. An investor could expect a yield of 7 per cent. Assuming an investor has a tax liability of 30p in £, then he could afford to purchase the interest at a price calculated as follows

Net income per annum   = £1000

YP for 10 years at 7 per cent and $2\frac{1}{2}$
per cent net (tax 30p in £)   = 5.063

Capital value   = £5063

(say)   £5050

If the investor is exempt from tax liabilities, he can afford to purchase the interest at a price calculated as follows.

A sinking fund of $2\frac{1}{2}$ per cent net was used in the previous calculation. The non-tax paying investor, however, can provide a sinking fund at the gross rate of interest, namely

Net rate × Gross adjustment factor

that is

$$2\frac{1}{2} \times \frac{1}{1-x} \left(\text{where } x = \frac{\text{tax rate in new pence}}{100} \right)$$

$$= 2\frac{1}{2} \times \frac{1}{1 - 0.30}$$

$$= 2\frac{1}{2} \times \frac{1}{0.70}$$

$$= 3.57 \text{ per cent}$$

$$(\text{say}) = 3\frac{1}{2} \text{ per cent}$$

(Annual Sinking Fund tables to $\frac{1}{4}$ per cent intervals) Then

Net income per annum   = £1000

YP for 10 years at 7 per cent and
$3\frac{1}{2}$ per cent gross =

$$\frac{1}{i+s} = \frac{1}{0.07 + \dfrac{0.035}{1.035^{10} - 1}}$$

$$= \frac{1}{0.07 + 0.0852} \qquad = \underline{6.44}$$

$$\text{Capital value} \qquad = \underline{£6440}$$

$$(\text{say}) \qquad\qquad = \underline{£6450}$$

The non-tax-paying investor could obtain a 7 per cent yield by purchasing the interest for £6450, whereas investors paying tax at 30p in £ could only afford to pay £5050.

If the non-tax paying investor is in competition with other investors, all having tax liabilities, he may purchase the interest by over-bidding his competitors, at a purchase price of say £5500. Hence, he would obtain a greater yield than 7 per cent. This may be calculated as follows

$$\text{YP} = \frac{\text{Purchase Price}}{\text{Net income per annum}} = \frac{£5500}{£1000} = 5.5$$

YP for 10 years at i per cent
and $3\frac{1}{2}$ per cent gross   = 5.5

$$5.5 = \frac{1}{i + 0.0852}$$

$$i = \frac{1 - (5.5 \times .00852)}{5.5}$$

$$= \frac{1 - 0.4686}{5.5} = \frac{0.5314}{5.5}$$

$$= 0.0966$$

$$= 9\tfrac{3}{4} \text{ per cent}$$

7.3 PROFIT RENT

Profit rent per annum is the difference between the rack rental value per annum and the rent paid per annum by an occupying lessee or sublessee on the same repairing and insuring terms.

Where a profit rent exists, the occupier has a saving on his annual expenses because he pays less for his occupation than the full rental value. This situation may occur because the lessee or sublessee has been in occupation for a period of time and his rent has not been reviewed recently, or he may have paid a premium at the commencement or during the period of his lease (see next section). When an occupier wishes to sell his lease or sublease, the profit rent per annum is capitalised to arrive at capital value.

Example. A shop is let on full repairing and insuring terms at a rent of £12 000 per annum, the lease having 12 years unexpired; the net rack rental value is £15 000 per annum. Value the leasehold interest.

Assuming a yield of 7 per cent and a tax liability of 30p in £

Net rack rental value per annum	= £15 000
Less Rent paid per annum	= £12 000
Profit rent per annum	= £3000

YP for 12 years at 7 per cent and
$2\frac{1}{2}$ per cent net (tax 30p in £)   =   5.762

                Capital value   = £17 286

                (say)   £17 300

The comparison between rack rental value and the rent paid must
be made when both are in relation to the same repairing and insuring terms. For example, it would be incorrect to compare a rent
paid under an internal repairing lease with a net rack rental value;
the rack rental value should be adjusted to internal repairing terms.
Table 7.1 illustrates how the rack rental value alters according to
differing repairing responsibilities incorporated in leases. The total

*Table 7.1   Calculation of Rack Rental Value in Relation to Differing Repair and
Insurance Responsibilities*

Assume that premises have a net rack rental value of £10 000 per annum;
it is estimated that external repairs will cost £1000 per annum, internal repairs
£500 per annum and insurance £50 per annum.
The table illustrates how the rack rental value of the premises varies,
according to differing repair and insurance responsibilities.

	Tenant is responsible for all repairs and insurance	Tenant has no respons- ibility for repairs and insurance	Tenant is responsible for external repairs and insurance only	Tenant is responsible for internal repairs only
Rack rental value per annum	£10 000	£11 550	£10 500	£11 050
Cost of external repairs per annum	£ 1 000	–	£ 1 000	–
Cost of internal repairs per annum	£ 500	–	–	£ 500
Cost of insurance per annum	£ 50	–	£ 50	–
Total cost to the tenant per annum of rent, repairs and insurance	£11 550	£11 550	£11 550	£11 550

annual cost to the tenant of rack rent and repair and insurance payments will be the same, irrespective of the division of repair and insurance responsibility.

Example. Premises are let on an internal repairing lease at £10 000 per annum. The net rack rental value is £12 000 per annum. Calculate the profit rent per annum.

The rack rental value is £12 000 per annum, when the tenant is responsible for all repairs and insurance. If the tenant is responsible for internal repairs only he would expect to pay a higher rent than £12 000, namely £12 000 plus external repairs and insurance (those items for which he is not responsible under the internal repairing lease). Thus adjusted rack rental value per annum = net rack rental value + cost of external repairs and insurance (say $12\frac{1}{2}$ per cent of net rack rental value) = £12 000 + £1500 = £13 500 per annum

Adjusted rack rental value per annum	= £13 500
Less Rent paid per annum on the same terms	= £10 000
Profit rent per annum	= £ 3 500

7.4 ERRORS IN MULTI-STAGE LEASEHOLD VALUATIONS

In the valuation of leasehold interests having varying profit rents, it is usual to apply a dual rate Years' Purchase, adjusted for tax.

This method assumes that the profit rents are valued separately, with separate sinking funds recouping original capital.

However, an investor would provide one constant sinking fund which would accumulate over the total unexpired period of the leasehold interest, recouping total capital value.

There appears to be a mathematical error in the method – does the annual sinking fund correctly replace the initial capital outlay?

Example. Value a profit rent of £1500 per annum for 3 years rising to be a profit rent of £2000 per annum for a further 5 years.

Assume a yield of 10 per cent, annual sinking fund of $2\frac{1}{2}$ per cent net, tax at 30p in £.

Profit rent per annum	= £1500
YP for 3 years at 10 per cent	

and $2\frac{1}{2}$ per cent net (tax 30p
in £)   =   1.771

                                                                £2656

Profit rent per annum   = £2000

YP for 5 years at 10 per cent
and $2\frac{1}{2}$ per cent net (tax 30p
in £)   = 2.69

PV of £1 in 3 years
at 10 per cent   = 0.751

YP for 5 years at 10 per cent
and $2\frac{1}{2}$ per cent net (tax
30p in £) deferred 3 years   =   2.02

                                                                £4040

                           Capital value   = £6696

                           (say)   £6700

A calculation will now be undertaken to assess whether or not
the annual sinking fund correctly replaces the initial capital outlay.

Spendable income – 10 per cent of £6700 = £670 per annum.

Profit rent per annum   = £1500

Less Spendable income per annum   = £ 670

                                                     £ 830

Less Tax at 30 per cent   = £ 249

                                                     £ 581

x Amount of £1 per annum for 3
years at $2\frac{1}{2}$ per cent   = 3.0756

                                                     £1786.92

x Amount of £1 for 5 years at
$2\frac{1}{2}$ per cent   = 1.1314

                 Capital replaced   = £2021.72

Reversion

Profit rent per annum   = £2000

Less Spendable income per annum $= \underline{\text{£ 670}}$

                                              £1330
Less Tax at 30 per cent $= \underline{\text{£ 399}}$

                                              £ 931

x Amount of £1 per annum for
5 years at $2\frac{1}{2}$ per cent $= \underline{5.2563}$

                    Capital replaced $= \underline{\text{£4893.62}}$

                    Total replaced capital $= \text{£6915.34}$

The total capital recouped is £6915 compared with an original capital outlay of £6700 – an over-provision of £215.

This over-provision may be rectified by the use of three methods, namely

(1) Double Sinking Fund Method
(2) Pannell's Method
(3) Annual Sinking Fund Method.

7.4.1 Double Sinking Fund Method

Using the previous example,

Let capital value $= x$

Profit rent per annum $= \text{£1500}$

Less annual sinking fund
to replace x in 8 years at $2\frac{1}{2}$
per cent net $= 0.114x$

Adjusted for tax at
30 per cent $= \underline{1.428}$

                                              $\underline{0.163x}$

Spendable income per annum $= \text{£1500} - 0.163x$

YP for 3 years at 10 per cent $= \underline{\quad 2.4869 \quad}$

                                  £3730 $- 0.405x$

Remaining 5 years

Profit rent per annum $= \text{£2000}$

Less annual sinking fund as before $= \underline{0.163x}$

Spendable income per annum $= \underline{\text{£2000} - 0.163x}$

YP for 5 years at
10 per cent $= 3.79$

PV of £1 in 3 years
at 10 per cent $= \underline{0.751}$

YP for 5 years at 10 per cent
deferred 3 years $= 2.846$

$$\frac{£5692 - 0464x}{£9422 - 0.869x}$$

Plus
* Repayment of capital replaced
by single rate sinking fund

$$x$$

PV of £1 in 8 years at 10
per cent $= 0.4665$

$$\frac{0.4665x}{}$$

Capital value $= £9422 - 0.4025x$

But capital value $= x$

So $x = £9422 - 0.4025x$

$1.4025x = £9422$

$$x = \frac{9422}{1.4025}$$

$$= £6718$$

*The capital has been replaced twice, at the accumulative rate of $2\frac{1}{2}$ per cent net (taxed) which is correct, and also at the rate of 10 per cent, because the Single Rate tables have a built-in sinking fund. The capital value of the interest has been excessively reduced, so that the deferred capital value is added back.

7.4.2 Pannell's Method

This is a 'short-cut' method; the profit rents are valued on a single rate basis. The resultant capital value is de-capitalised to obtain an *annual equivalent*. This is then re-capitalised with a dual rate taxed Years' Purchase.

Profit rent per annum $= £1500$

YP for 3 years at 10 per cent   = 2.4869

                                        £3731

Profit rent per annum   = £2000

YP for 5 years at
10 per cent   = 3.79

PV of £1 in 3 years
at 10 per cent   = 0.75

YP for 5 years at 10 per cent
deferred 3 years   = 2.8425

                                        £5685

Capital value on single rate basis   = £9416

Annual Equivalent = $\dfrac{£9416}{\text{YP for 8 years at 10 per cent}}$

$= \dfrac{9416}{5.3349} = £1765 \text{ per annum}$

Constant rent per annum   = £1765

YP for 8 years at 10 per cent
and $2\frac{1}{2}$ per cent net (tax 30p
in £)   = 3.795

            Capital value   = £6698

7.4.3 Sinking Fund Method

Let capital value   = x

Spendable income = $0.10x$

Profit rent per annum   = £1500

Less Spendable income per annum   = $\dfrac{0.10x}{£1500 - 0.10x}$

Less Tax at 30 per cent   = $\dfrac{£450 - 0.03x}{£1050 - 0.07x}$

$\times$ Amount of £1 per annum for
3 years at $2\frac{1}{2}$ per cent
                = 3.0756

$\times$ Amount of £1 for 5

years at $2\frac{1}{2}$ per cent

$$= \underline{1.1314} \qquad \underline{3.48}$$

$$= £3654 - 0.2436x$$

Profit rent per annum	$= £2000$
Less Spendable income per annum	$= \underline{0.10x}$
	$£2000 - 0.10x$
Less Tax at 30 per cent	$= \underline{£\ 600\ -\ 0.03x}$
	$£1400 - 0.07x$
$\times$ Amount of £1 per annum for 5 years at $2\frac{1}{2}$ per cent	$= \underline{5.2563}$
	$£7359 - 0.3679x$
Capital value	$= £11\,013 - 0.6115x$

But capital value $= x$

$x = £11\,013 - 0.6115x$

$1.6115x = £11\,013$

$x = \underline{11\,013}$
1.6115
$ = £6834$

In summary:

	Capital Value
Traditional Method	£6700
Double Sinking Fund Method	£6718
Pannell's Method	£6698
Sinking Fund Method	£6834

For further consideration of these methods, reference, may be made to Diane Butler, *Applied Valuation* (Macmillan, 1987).

7.5 PREMIUMS

A premium is a sum of money that is paid by a lessee at the commencement, or during the period, of a lease in consideration of a reduction in rent. The lessee purchases an annual profit rent and the landlord capitalises a part of his future income. The landlord receives a capital sum for immediate investment, which may be partially tax-free, and the security of his annual income is increased. The premium may have the effect of increasing the landlord's confidence in his tenant where consents are required under the lease, such as permission to alter or improve the premises.

7.5.1 Calculation of the Premium or Reduction in Rent

A lessee may request a specified deduction in rent per annum upon the granting of a lease; the premium to be paid should be equivalent to the capital value of the annual profit rent.

Example. A lessee has been granted a 14-year lease of a shop having a net rack rental value of £15 000 per annum. He has agreed to pay £10 000 per annum, subject to the immediate payment of a premium. Calculate the premium.

Assuming a yield of 7 per cent and a tax liability of 30p in £

Net rack rental value per annum	= £15 000
Less Rent to be paid per annum	= £10 000
Profit rent per annum	= £ 5 000
YP for 14 years at 7 per cent and $2\frac{1}{2}$ per cent net (tax 30p in £)	= 6.39
Premium	= £31 950

Alternatively the premium may be agreed and the reduction in rent per annum has to be calculated. The lessee will forgo a capital sum, and he will expect in return a reduction in rent totalling

    (i) the interest forgone on the premium at the leasehold rate of interest, i and
    (ii) a sum sufficient to recover the initial capital outlay by means of a sinking fund (adjusted for tax liabilities) at the time the lease expires, $s(1/1 - x)$, so that the total is

$$i + s\left(\frac{1}{1 - x}\right)$$

This is the annual equivalent of the premium, or the Annuity £1 will Purchase (see Chapter 5).

The reduction in rent may be calculated as

Premium × Annuity £1 will purchase

or more conveniently

$$\frac{\text{Premium}}{\text{YP for the term of the lease}}$$

Example. A shop is to be let on a 14-year full repairing and insuring lease having a net rack rental value of £12 000 per annum. The tenant has agreed to pay a premium of £20 000 at the commencement of the lease. Calculate the rent per annum to be paid. Assuming a yield of 7 per cent and a tax liability of 30p in £

Net rack rental value   = £12 000

Less Reduction in rent

Annual equivalent of the premium

$$= \frac{20000}{\text{YP for 14 years at 7 per cent and } 2\frac{1}{2} \text{ per cent net (tax 30p in £)}}$$

$= \dfrac{20000}{6.39}$ = £3130

Rent to be paid per annum   = £8870

There may be instances where the tenant agrees to pay a premium at a future date. In order to calculate the reduction in rent per annum, the present cost of the future premium may be determined and the annual equivalent then found.

Example. A tenant has been granted a 14-year full repairing and insuring lease of premises having a net rack rental value per annum of £20 000. The tenant has agreed to pay a premium of £30 000 in 5 years' time. Calculate the rent per annum he should pay, assuming a yield of 8 per cent and a tax liability of 30p in £.

Net rack rental value per annum   = £20 000

Less Reduction in rent

Present cost of premium =

£30 000 x PV of £1 in 5 years at $2\frac{1}{2}$ per cent

£30 000 x 0.884 = £26 520

$$\text{Annual equivalent} = \frac{£26\,520}{\text{YP for 14 years at 8 per cent and } 2\frac{1}{2} \text{ per cent net (tax 30p in £)}}$$

$$= \frac{£26\,520}{6.01} \qquad\qquad = \underline{£\ 4\,413}$$

Rent to be paid per annum $= £15\,587$

Where a tenant has a liability to pay a premium at a known future date, he may provide for this by investing a capital sum or by an annual sinking fund. In either case, the rate of interest for investment to provide the capital sum should be a low risk-free rate, that is, an accumulative rate of interest such as $2\frac{1}{2}$ or 3 per cent net.

Example. Considering the previous example, where a tenant agreed to pay a premium of £30 000 in 5 years' time, this may be provided by investment of an initial capital sum or an annual sinking fund.

  (i) Initial capital sum = £30 000 × PV of £1 in 5 years at $2\frac{1}{2}$ per cent
                = £30 000 × 0.884 = £26 520
 (ii) Annual sinking fund = £30 000 × Annual sinking fund to
                provide £1 in 5 years at $2\frac{1}{2}$ per cent
                = £30 000 x 0.190 = £5700

(*Note* The value of the future premium to the landlord at the commencement of the lease is £30 000 deferred by a remunerative rate of interest; that is, £30 000 × PV of £1 in 5 years at 8 per cent = £30 000 × 0.681 = £20 430. It is usual, however, to calculate the premium or rent from the tenant's viewpoint.)

7.6 COMBINED FREEHOLD AND LEASEHOLD VALUATIONS

A characteristic of land and property is that there may exist at the same time freehold, leasehold and subleasehold interests, all having capital values.

A valuer may be required to calculate the value of each of these interests.

Example. A is the freeholder of a shop let to *B* on an internal repairing lease, having 8 years unexpired at a rent of £10 000 per annum. *B* sublet the shop last year to *C* on a 5 year internal repairing lease at a rent of £15 000 per annum.

The current net rack rental value is considered to be £16 000 per annum.

Value the interests of *A, B* and *C.*

A's interest Assuming a freehold yield on rack rental value terms to be 8 per cent.

Unexpired term of lease is 8 years

Rent received per annum	= £10 000	
Less External repairs and insurance say $12\frac{1}{2}$ per cent of net rack rent	= £ 2 000	
Net income per annum	= £ 8 000	
YP for 8 years at 15 per cent	= 4.487	
		£ 35 896

Reversion

Net rack rental value per annum	= £16 000	
YP in perpetuity deferred 8 years at 8 per cent	= 6.753	
		= £108 048
Capital value		= £143 944
(Say)		= £143 950

B's interest Assuming leasehold yield to be 9 per cent on rack rental value terms and tax liability to be 30p in £.

First 4 years

Rent received per annum	= £15 000
Less Rent paid per annum	= £10 000
Net income per annum	= £ 5 000

YP for 4 years at 9 per cent
and $2\frac{1}{2}$ per cent net,
(tax 30p in £)   = 2.304

£11 520

Second 4 years

Reversion to adjusted rack
rental value per annum
(under the head lease B
is responsible for internal
repairs only, so that this
is the only repair liability
he would impose on a
sublessee). Hence adjusted
rack rental value per annum =
£16 000 + external repairs
and insurance =
£16 000 + £2000   = £18 000

Less Rent paid per annum   = £10 000

Net income per annum   = £ 8 000

YP for 4 years at 9 per cent
and $2\frac{1}{2}$ per cent net (tax 30p
in £)   = 2.304

PV of £1 in 4 years
at 9 per cent   = 0.708

YP for 4 years at 9 per cent
and $2\frac{1}{2}$ per cent net (tax
30p in £) deferred 4 years   = 1.631

£13 048

Capital value   = £24 568

(say)   = £24 600

C's interest Assuming subleasehold yield to be 9   per cent and tax
liability to be 30p in £.

Adjusted rack rental value

per annum   = £18 000

Less Rent paid per annum	= £15 000	
Profit rent per annum	= £ 3 000	
YP for 4 years at $9\frac{1}{2}$ per cent and $2\frac{1}{2}$ per cent net (tax 30p in £)	= 2.278	
Capital value		= £6834
(say)		= £6850

Example. X is the freeholder of land, which was let to Y 30 years ago on a 99 year ground lease at a fixed rent of £1000 per annum. Shop premises were built on the land, and these have a current net rack rental value of £25 000 per annum. 11 years ago, Y sublet the shop to Z on a 21 year internal repairing lease at a rent of £15 000 per annum.

Value the interests of X, Y and Z.

X's interest Assuming that the freehold yield for a ground rent with long-term fixed income (very *inflation-prone*) is 20 per cent, and for shop premises is 8 per cent.

Ground rent per annum	= £1000	
YP for 69 years at 20 per cent	= 5	
		£5000

Reversion

Net rack rental value per annum	= £25 000	
YP in perpetuity deferred 69 years at 8 per cent	= 0.062	
		= £1550
Capital value		= £6550

(*Note* It may be argued that the reversion is too far distant to be valued and the valuation may be:

Ground rent per annum	= £1000	
YP in perpetuity at 20 per cent	= 5	
Capital value	= £5000)	

Y's interest Assuming a leasehold yield of 9 per cent and a tax liability of 30p in £.

Unexpired term of sublease is 10 years

Rent received per annum	= £15 000

Less Ground rent per annum = £ 1 000

External repairs and insurance
say $12\frac{1}{2}$ per cent of net rack
rent £25 000   = £3125   = £ 4 125

Net income per annum   = £10 875

YP for 10 years at 9 per cent
and $2\frac{1}{2}$ per cent net (tax
30p in £)   = 4.597

                                   £49 992

Remaining 59 years

Reversion to net rack rental
value per annum   = £25 000

Less Ground rent per annum   = £ 1 000

Net income per annum   = £24 000

YP for 59 years at 9 per cent
and $2\frac{1}{2}$ per cent net (tax 30p
in £)   = 9.916

PV of £1 in 10 years
at 9 per cent   = 0.422

YP for 59 years at 9 per cent and
$2\frac{1}{2}$ per cent (tax 30p in
£) deferred 10 years   = 4.185

                                   £100 440

             Capital value   = £150 432

                 (say)   = £150 450

Z's interest Assuming a subleasehold yield of 10 per cent and a tax liability of 30p in £.

Adjusted rack rental value per annum =
Net rack rental value per annum + external repairs and insurance
= £25 000 + £3125 = £28 125.

Adjusted rack rental value per annum	=	£28 125
Less Rent paid per annum	=	£15 000
Profit rent per annum	=	£13 125
YP for 10 years at 10 per cent and $2\frac{1}{2}$ per cent net (tax 30p in £)	=	4.395
Capital value	=	£57 684
(say)	=	£57 700

7.7 PURCHASERS WITH A SPECIAL INTEREST

A purchaser with a special interest may be one who can afford to pay more for the purchase of a legal estate than other investors, because of the creation of *marriage value.*

Marriage value will occur if:

(i) two or more legal interests are merged in the same property.

Example. A freehold property is occupied by a lessee, and he now wishes to purchase the freehold interest. He can afford to pay more for the interest than other investors, because he will cancel out the existence of his own leasehold interest.

(ii) two or more adjacent pieces of land in separate ownerships are merged into one ownership.

Marriage value will 'be created in either case if the value of the single, merged interest exceeds the total of the values of the separate interests before the merger' (Andrew Baum and Gary Sams, *Statutory Valuations* (Routledge and Kegan Paul, 1990)).

Example. Nos 1, 2 and 3 Church Street are shops with living accommodation over, details of which are shown below:

Shop No.	Freeholder	Net rack rental value per annum	Occupier and type of shop	Details of any lease
1.	C. Dickens	£3000	C. Dickens (Grocer)	
2.	T. Hardy	£3500	W. Wordsworth (Gardening equipment)	Let to Wordsworth on an internal repairing lease with 5 years unexpired at a rent of £2500 per annum.
3.	W. Shakespeare	£3300	E. Blyton (Book shop)	Let to Blyton on an internal repairing lease with 10 years unexpired at a rent of £3000 per annum.

C. Dickens has ambitious plans to take his brother-in-law into partnership and extend his business into a supermarket. This will necessitate obtaining the unencumbered freehold interests of shops 2 and 3, Church Street. The shops would cost £25 000 to alter and convert, giving a net rack rental value of £16 000 per annum for the supermarket.

Value all the interests, and advise Dickens as to the gain he will enjoy by the merger of the interests.

Value of the supermarket

Assuming a freehold yield of 7 per cent.

Net rack rental value per annum	= £16 000
YP in perpetuity at 7 per cent	= 14.28
	£228 480
Less Cost of alteration and conversion	= £ 25 000
Capital value	= £203 480
(say)	= £203 500

Shop No. 1

C. Dickens' interest.

Assuming a freehold yield, when let at a net rack rent of 8 per cent.

Net rack rental value per annum	= £ 3 000	
YP in perpetuity at 8 per cent	= 12.5	
Capital value	= £37 500	

Shop No. 2

T. Hardy's interest.
Assuming a freehold yield, when let at a net rack rental of 8 per cent.

Unexpired term of lease is 5 years

Rent received per annum	= £2500	
Less External repairs and insurance say $12\frac{1}{2}$ per cent of net rack rent £3 500		
(say)	= £ 440	
Net income per annum	= £2060	
YP for 5 years at 15 per cent	= 3.352	
		£ 6 905

Reversion

Net rack rental value per annum	= £3500	
YP in perpetuity deferred 5 years at 8 per cent	= 8.507	
		£29 774
Capital value		= £36 679
(say)		£36 700

W. Wordsworth's interest.
Assuming a leasehold yield of 9 per cent and a tax liability of 30p in £.
Adjusted rack rental value per annum =
net rack rental value per annum + external repairs and insurance = £3500 + £440   = £3940

Less Rent paid per annum	= £2500
Profit rent per annum	= £1440

YP for 5 years at 9 per cent and $2\frac{1}{2}$ per cent net (tax 30p in £)	=	<u>2.764</u>
Capital value	=	<u>£3980</u>
(say)	=	<u>£4000</u>

Shop No. 3

W. Shakespeare's interest

Assuming a freehold yield, when let at a net rack rent, of 8 per cent.

Unexpired term of lease is 10 years Rent received per annum	=	£3000
Less External repairs and insurance say $12\frac{1}{2}$ per cent of net rack rent, £3300 say	=	<u>£ 400</u>
Net income per annum	=	£2600
YP for 10 years at 15 per cent	=	<u>5.019</u>
		£13 049

Reversion

Net rack rental value per annum	=	£3300
YP in perpetuity deferred 10 years at 8 per cent	=	<u>5.79</u>
		<u>£19 107</u>
Capital value	=	<u>£32 156</u>
(say)	=	<u>£32 150</u>

E. Blyton's interest

Assuming a yield of 9 per cent and a tax liability of 30p in £.
Adjusted rack rental value per annum =
Net rack rental value per annum + external repairs and

insurance = £3300 + 400	=	<u>£3700</u>
Less Rent paid per annum	=	<u>£3000</u>
Profit rent per annum	=	£ 700

YP for 10 years at 9 per cent
and $2\frac{1}{2}$ per cent net (tax 30p
in £)   = <u>4.597</u>

         Capital value   = <u>£3218</u>

         (say)   = £3200

Summary

Value of the supermarket	= £203 500

Less

C. Dickens' interest	= £37 500
T. Hardy's interest	= £36 700
W. Wordsworth's interest	= £ 4 000
W. Shakespeare's interest	= £32 150
E. Blyton's interest	= <u>£ 3 200</u>
	£113 550
Marriage value	= £ 89 950

Dickens will enjoy a gain on the merger of the interests of £89 950. He can use this surplus to 'over-bid' any other investors who may wish to purchase the interests in shops 2 and 3. In practice, it is likely that he will only use a proportion of the marriage value to obtain the unencumbered freehold of nos 2 and 3, thus giving him the opportunity to carry out the supermarket scheme.

QUESTIONS

7.1 A small modern office building well situated in the centre of a city is occupied by the head lessee on a lease having 49 years unexpired at a ground rent of £750 per annum. The current net rack rental value is £25 000 per annum. The freeholder has decided to sell his interest.
(i) Value the freehold and leasehold interests.
(ii) Calculate the marriage gain, which the lessee will enjoy if the freehold is purchased by him.

7.2 *X* is the owner of a freehold interest in a shop which has a current net rack rental value of £12 000 per annum. 14 years ago, *X* let the shop to *Y* on a 21 year lease on full repairing insuring terms at a rent of £5000 per annum, subject to the payment of a premium of £3000. 11 years ago, *Y* sublet the premises to *Z* on a 14 year internal repairing and insuring lease at a rent of £7000 per annum. *Z* paid a premium of £4000.

Value the interests of *X*, *Y* and *Z*.

7.3 *A* is the freeholder of a site with a small office building upon it. 34 years ago, *A* let the site to *B* (who built the offices) on a 99 year ground lease at a fixed rent of £1000 per annum. 7 years ago, *B* sublet to *C* on a 21 year internal repairing lease at a rent of £4000 per annum. 5 years ago, *C* sublet to *D* for 7 years at a rent of £6000 per annum, *D* having no responsibility for repairs.

The current net rack rental value of the office building is considered to be £8000 per annum.

Value all interests.

7.4 5 years ago, a small modern freehold factory was let on a 21 year full repairing and insuring lease. The lessee is liable to pay an extra year's rent at the end of the 7th and 14th years in addition to the £7000 per annum reserved in the lease.

The freeholder is liable to pay £3000 to the former owner in 2 years' time in respect of a surface water drain.

The current net rack rental value is £12 000 per annum.

Value the freehold and leasehold interests.

7.5 4 years ago, a firm of investment analysts was granted a 20 year lease of a small office block, the lease having 5 year rent reviews. The commencing rent was £30 000 per annum, and the firm are responsible for all outgoings which are paid by a service charge.

Last year, business was disappointing and with the landlord's consent, the firm sublet 25 per cent of the net lettable space to a firm of accountants at a commencing rent of £9000 per annum, the accountants paying their portion of the service charge. The sublease provides for rent reviews after 1 year, 6 years and 11 years to ensure that reviews for both head lease and sublease coincide.

Rental values have increased by $5\frac{1}{2}$ per cent during the past year.

Value all interests.

7.6 Value the following leasehold investment using

   (i) a traditional method
   (ii) Double Sinking Fund Method
   (iii) Pannell's Method
   (iv) Annual Sinking Fund Method -

A profit rent of £3000 per annum for 4 years, rising to £5000 per annum for a further 4 years.

   Assume a yield of 8 per cent, annual sinking fund at $2\frac{1}{2}$ per cent net and tax at 30p in £.

8 Methods of Valuation

The valuer is often required to calculate the capital and rental values of properties of different tenures and types. There are various methods of valuation that may be used and these will be explained in this chapter.

8.1 THE INVESTMENT METHOD

This has been considered in previous chapters and consists of capitalising the net income which a property produces, namely

Net income per annum × Years' Purchase = Capital value

The suitability of the method depends upon a variety of factors, including the use of a realistic yield, an accurate allowance for outgoings and, in the case of leasehold interests, an appropriate tax rate.

8.2 THE COMPARISON METHOD

One method of deciding the value of a property is to compare it with similar properties for which transactions have already taken place. This procedure is widely adopted in practice, but requires the keeping of adequate records of transactions.

Professional offices should record all details of property dealings with which they are involved, so that this information is available for future reference. The valuer should keep up-to-date with the property market by reading technical and professional journals.

A comparison method may be used for assessing the rental value of a particular property; the unit of comparison in commercial and industrial property may be the square metre of net floor area and, in agricultural land, the hectare.

A 'zoning' method may be used for obtaining rental values of shops. Shops having the same floor area and condition and being in the same locality may not have the same rental value. This may be due to varying lengths of frontage. The zoning method takes account of this by assuming that the front area of a shop has greater value than the rear portion.

The method splits the depth of the shop into zones, and assumes that the value per m² *halves back* from the front zone. The depth of the zones must be established at the outset – the usual practice may be 6.10 metres (the front zone referred to as *Zone A*), 6.10 metres (second zone – *Zone B*) and a remainder (this equates to two 20 feet zones and a remainder). A zoning pattern of 4.57 m *Zone A*, 7.62 m *Zone B* and a remainder (15 feet/25 feet and a remainder) is also used in practice.

Example. A shop having a frontage of 8 m and a depth of 16 m has recently been let at a rent of £76 800 per annum, on full repairing and insuring terms. Analyse this rent to calculate the annual rental value of a similar shop in the same locality, having a frontage of 10 m and a depth of 18 m.

Analysing the rent of £76 800 per annum: assume that the depth of the shop is split from the front into two 6.10 m zones, leaving a balance of 3.80 m. The value of the second zone is assumed to be 50 per cent of the front zone and the rear zone 50 per cent of the second zone. (It is usual to divide the depth into three zones only). So that if the rent per square metre of the front zone is assumed to be £x, the rental value will be

Front zone – *Zone A* 8 m × 6.10 m × x $= 48.8x$

Second zone – *Zone B* 8 m × 6.10 m × $0.5x$ $= 24.4x$

Rear zone – *remainder* 8 m × 3.80 m × $0.25x$ $= \underline{7.6x}$

$$80.8x$$

$80.8x = £76\ 800$

$$x = \frac{76\ 800}{80.8} = £950.49/m^2$$

(say) £950/m² ITZA ~~Rental value~~

(*Note* ITZA = In terms of *Zone A*.)

Taking the information supplied and adopting the principles used in the analysis, the annual rental value of the second shop will be

Zone A = 10 m × 6.10 m × £950 = £57 950

Zone B = 10 m × 6.10 m × £475 = £28 975

Remainder = 10 m × 5.80 m × £237.5 = £13 775

Annual rental value = £100 700

Care must be taken as to how frontage and depth are measured and guidance is given in the *Code of Measuring Practice* produced by the Royal Institution of Chartered Surveyors and the Incorporated Society of Valuers and Auctioneers (1993).

The comparison method may be used for calculating capital values by analysing transactions of similar properties to find the appropriate yields. These may be applied to value other properties.

Example. A freehold factory has recently been sold for £300 000. The 21 year full repairing and insuring lease has 9 years unexpired and has provision for rent reviews every 7 years. The rent passing is £25 000 per annum, and the current net rack rental value is considered to be £27 500 per annum.

Analyse this sale and apply the results to value similar premises let on a 21 year internal repairing lease, having 3 years unexpired, at a rent of £30 000 per annum. The net rack rental value is considered to be £32 000 per annum.

The recent sale may be analysed to obtain the yield applicable to the income obtainable from the first review onwards.

Assuming the yield for the first 2 years to be 15 per cent and the unknown yield *i*:

Term to the first rent review is 2 years

Rent received per annum = £25 000

YP for 2 years at 15 per cent = 1.626 $\dfrac{1}{(1+0.15)^2}$

£40 650

First Rent Review

Net rack rental value per annum = £27 500

YP in perpetuity deferred 2
years at i x

                                       $27\,500x$

Capital value (given)   £300 000

Therefore, £300 000 = £40 650 + £27 500x

$$x = \frac{300\,000 - 40\,650}{27\,500}$$

$x = 9.43$

YP in perpetuity deferred 2 years at i 9.43

Using *Parry's Valuation and Investment Tables.*

Look up the Years' Purchase of a Reversion to a Perpetuity table across the 2 year line; the nearest YP figure to 9.43 is 9.352 i.e. a yield of 9 per cent.
Applying the results:

Unexpired term of lease is 3 years

Rent received per annum   = £30 000

Less External repairs and insurance
say 12½ per cent of net rack
                 rent £32 000   = £ 4 000

Net income per annum   = £26 000

YP for 3 years at 15 per cent   = 2.283

                                             £59 358

Reversion

Net rack rental value per annum   = £32 000

YP in perpetuity deferred 3 years at
           9 per cent   = 8.58

                                             £274 560

                     Capital value = £333 918

                     (say)   = £333 900

If the valuation of the leasehold interest is required:

Adjusted rack rent per annum = Net
Rack rental value per annum + external repairs and insurance =
£32 000 + £4000 = £36 000

Assuming a yield of 10 per cent and a tax liability of 30p in £:

Adjusted rack rental value per annum	= £36 000
Less Rent paid per annum	= £30 000
Profit rent per annum	= £ 6 000
YP for 3 years at 10 per cent and $2\frac{1}{2}$ per cent net (tax 30p in £)	= 1.771
Capital value	= £10 626
(say)	= £10 650

8.3   THE RESIDUAL METHOD

This method may be used to value land that is to be developed or redeveloped. It is essential to ascertain the uses for which planning permission could be obtained and to prepare an outline scheme for development or redevelopment of the site. There may be a number of alternative schemes, in which case it is necessary to determine which will give the greatest return. The method depends upon making an estimate of the value of the land when developed or improved and deducting from this the costs of construction and site works, architect's and quantity surveyor's fees, legal fees, estate agency and advertising costs, interest on capital borrowed, contingencies and developer's profits. The residue is the value of the site.

Example. Calculate the site value of land which has planning permission for 7000 m² (gross external area) of office space. The development will be completed within 2 years and it is anticipated that rents will be £125 per m² of net internal area. Reduce gross external area to net internal area – deduct say 20 per cent = 1400 m².

Net internal area = 5600 m² × £125	= £ 700 000
YP in perpetuity at 8 per cent	= 12.5
Gross Development Value	= £8 750 000
Less Site preparation, say	£ 10 000

Cost of building 7000 m² x £600/m²	= £4 200 000
Contingencies say 10 per cent	= £ 420000

421 000 was written originally but this is wrong

Architects' and quantity surveyors' fees, say 10 per cent of cost and contingencies	= £ 463 100

Also wrong should be 462000 Correct.

Financing – 2 years at 12 per cent and ½ of £5 094 100 = (1.12² × 2 547 050) − 2 547 050	= £647 969
Legal costs, advertising and estate agency fees, say 3 per cent of value	= £262 500
Developer's profit, say 10 per cent of value	= £875 000
	£6 879 569
Residue =	1 870 431

This residue represents three items: the value of the land; acquisition costs, say 4 per cent of value; and the cost of borrowing for 2 years at 12 per cent per annum on land value and costs.

Residue   £1 870 431 = $(x + 0.04x) \times 1.12^2$

where x = land value
£1 870 431 = 1.3046x

Site value   = $\dfrac{£1\,870\,431}{1.3046}$ = £1 433 720

(say)   £1 433 700

Notes

(i) Fees are based on the assumption that professional scales of fees are applied; the developer may, however, employ his own professional staff, who are paid salaries.

(ii) It is assumed that capital would be borrowed for 2 years only at a rate of 12 per cent per annum. Some developers may, however, finance the development with income derived from other schemes, but they would expect some return for the use of this income.

(iii) Contingencies are included to allow for such items as emergencies and increased building costs.

(iv) The rate of profit will vary from developer to developer and from scheme to scheme.

This method is often used by valuers to advise clients on the potential value of their land, but the Lands Tribunal is very reluctant to accept it, because of the many variable factors involved in the calculation. Relatively small differences in approach in individual parts of the valuation can produce considerable variations in the final answer. The Lands Tribunal will only accept the method if there is no more suitable method of valuation available.

A valuer may feel confident in using the method when advising a client as to the amount he can afford to bid when wishing to buy development land. He must be aware of his client's facility for borrowing capital, profit requirements and availability of an organisation for carrying out the development.

8.4 THE PROFITS OR ACCOUNTS METHOD

This method of valuation is applicable to special properties such as hotels and public houses, cinemas, theatres and fairgrounds. The value in these cases is wholly or partly dependent on a capacity to earn income on occupation of the property.

The calculation requires the estimation of the average annual gross earnings of the property and the deduction from this figure of the working expenses (excluding rent) and an amount for the occupier's remuneration, including interest on the capital he has 'tied up' in the business. The balance represents the amount available for annual rent, which is then capitalised by an appropriate Years' Purchase to arrive at capital value.

Example. Calculate the value of a 'free' public house (that is, not tied to a brewery) having a bar and catering trade and shortly to be offered on lease.

A typical valuation might be

Receipts from bar and food   £80 000

Less Working expenses and occupier's remuneration	£20 000
Purchases	£30 000
Interest on capital of £30 000 (furniture, fittings and equipment, stock and cash) – allow 8 per cent	£ 2 400
	£52 400
Profits per annum	£27 600

Assume that a tenant would be prepared to pay 40 per cent of profit as rent, that is, 40 per cent of £27 600 = £11 040. Hence

Rent per annum	= £11 040
YP in perpetuity at 12 per cent	= 8.334
Capital value	= £92 007
(say)	£92 000

(*Note* Interest on capital – the £50 000 employed in the business could have been invested elsewhere at a remunerative rate of interest such as 8 per cent.)

This method, used mainly for rating purposes, should be checked by other methods where possible. Comparables may be obtained on the basis of annual rent per cinema seat or hotel bedroom. Valuation of these types of property requires a specialist skill.

8.5 THE REINSTATEMENT METHOD

This method requires the estimation of the cost of rebuilding a particular property and adding to it the value of the land on which it stands.

Example. Calculate the value of a house having a gross area of 100 m^2 standing on land having a site value of £50 000.

Cost of reinstatement: 100 m^2 at £600/m^2	= £ 60 000
Architect's and other fees say 10 per cent	= £ 6 000
Value of land	= £ 50 000
Capital value	= £116 000

This method may be used for fire-insurance purposes to calculate the annual premium. It may appear that the premium need only be based on £66 000, because the site would remain even if the property was destroyed. However, it may be practical to insure for the complete value of £116 000. If property is partially destroyed and is 'written off' by an insurance company, there may be demolition costs to be paid. These may be paid by the insurance company because of the £50 000 site value taken into account in the insured sum. For example

Value of building 'written off'	= £66 000
Demolition of remaining portions	= £ 3 000
Insurance paid	= £69 000

8.6   THE CONTRACTOR'S METHOD

This method is similar to the reinstatement method, but is applied to those specialised properties such as town halls, colleges, sewage-disposal works and broiler houses that do not normally come on the market. The capital value is found by calculating the cost of building the property and adding to this the value of the site. This method may be used for rating purposes. The capital value is decapitalised to arrive at a reasonable rent, which is then used for determining the gross and rateable values of the property.

The method is difficult to apply to old buildings because there may be unusable and obsolescent parts. In these cases, it is usual to base the capital value on the cost of a substituted building of similar size and using modern building materials. A deduction is then made for age and obsolescence. This allowance varies considerably and provides, in many cases, an inaccurate method of calculation. For rating purposes a percentage of the capital value is taken to represent rent. This has varied from $3\frac{1}{2}$ per cent in the case of universities to 5 per cent in the case of broiler houses.

Example. College buildings, built 100 years ago, are in a dilapidated condition; substituted buildings would cost £1 000 000 to build. Assess a reasonable rent per annum.

Capital cost of new building	= £1 000 000
Less Disability allowance on account of age and obsolescence, say 70 per cent	= £ 700 000
Effective capital value	= £ 300 000

Plus Value of land   = £   50 000

                                                        = £   350 000

                                  4 per cent   0.04

            Reasonable rent per annum   = £   14 000

The method requires extreme care when assessing allowances for age and the percentages. The Lands Tribunal prefers valuations based on comparables of rentals, but will accept this method if more specific information is not available.

Valuations of properties, where there is no market for sale, often need to be incorporated in the accounts of companies. In these situations, *Statements of Asset Valuation Practice and Guidance Notes*, prepared by the Royal Institution of Chartered Surveyors, recommend the *Depreciated Replacement Cost Basis of Valuation*.

This basis is a variation of the Contractor's Method and is the sum of:

(a) the open market value of the land for its existing use, plus

(b) the current gross replacement cost of the buildings and their site works less an allowance for all appropriate factors such as age, condition, functional and environmental obsolescence which result in the existing property being worth less than a new replacement.

The method may be used to value specialist properties such as oil refineries, power stations and museums.

Example. Buildings, part of an oil refinery complex, have a gross external area of 2200 m² and were built 22 years ago.

It is assumed that they have a useful economic life of 50 years from new.

Valuation

(i) The value of the land would be obtained by comparables based upon the most appropriate alternative use. In this situation, this might be heavy industrial use.

(ii) The value of the buildings would be obtained by using the *depreciated replacement cost* method.

        Gross replacement cost –
        2200 m² × say £600/m²   = £1 320 000

Add Professional fees $12\frac{1}{2}$ per cent   =   165 000
                                                    £1 485 000

Plus Value Added Tax, $17\frac{1}{2}$ per cent   =   259 875

Gross Replacement Cost   = £1 744 875

This figure is now reduced to a Net Replacement Cost by allowing for depreciation on a straight-line basis.

i.e. Net Replacement Cost =

Gross Replacement Cost $\times \dfrac{\text{Years Remaining}}{\text{Total life in years}}$

$= £1\,744\,875 \times \dfrac{28}{50}$

$= £977\,130$

The figure of £977 130 would be incorporated in the balance sheet separate from the land value, as the building is a depreciable asset and the land a perpetual asset.

Further reference may be made to Diane Butler and David Richmond, *Advanced Valuation* (Macmillan, 1990).

QUESTIONS

8.1 A freehold office building was recently sold for £477 500. It was let 3 years ago on a 5 year full repairing and insuring lease at a rent of £30 000 per annum. Its current net rack rental value is £40 000 per annum.

Analyse this transaction and apply the results to value the freehold and leasehold interests in a three-storey office building. The freeholder occupies the ground floor but has let the two upper floors on internal repairing terms at a rent of £24 000 per annum, the lease having 3 years unexpired. The current net rack rental value of the whole building is considered to be £50 000 per annum. Each floor has the same net internal area but the current net rack rental value of each of the upper floors is 75 per cent of that of the ground floor.

8.2 Value all the interests in the following shop which has a frontage of 6 m and a depth of 20 m.

2 years ago, the freeholder let the shop on a 15 year internal repairing lease, with rent reviews every 5 years, at a rent of £60 000 per annum.

A similar shop, with a frontage of 7 m and a depth of 17 m, was recently let on a 5 year full repairing and insuring lease for £72 500 per annum and then sold for £1 035 500.

8.3 Your client is the freeholder of 7000 m² of land which has planning consent for light industrial development. The consent would permit a maximum site coverage of 40 per cent. Approximately 10 per cent of the floor space will be office accommodation, the remainder being production area. Finance is available at 12 per cent per annum.

Using your own figures, calculate the value of the freehold site on behalf of your client.

9 Inflation and Growth

The investment method for valuing freehold and leasehold interests described earlier is limited in handling change in the level of net rental incomes. This change may be due to inflation in the economy which causes the purchasing power of money to deteriorate. The supply and demand for property may also change in real terms.

The ability of the net income from property to fluctuate to take account of these factors depends upon whether it is 'fixed' or 'variable'. If income is fixed over a long period of time it is 'inflation-prone'; if, however, it varies according to change it is 'inflation proof' (income receivable under a lease with regular rent reviews may be considered reasonably 'inflation-proofed').

In a traditional valuation, the valuer normally adjusts the remunerative yield for discounting future income and costs to take account of anticipated value change. This might be termed 'initial yield' or 'all risks yield' and is basically net income expressed as a percentage of capital value.

A 'real value' approach may be adopted for valuing incomes in fluctuating circumstances and two other types of yield may be used:

(1) 'equated' yield, which is the true yield on an investment taking into account possible appreciation or depreciation during its life, and
(2) 'inflation risk free yield' (IRFY) which can be used to value the income from an investment rising to meet any reduction in the value of the income caused by inflation.

9.1.1 Valuation Methods

Assume that an income currently £5000 per annum, subject to 5 year rent reviews, is to be valued in perpetuity. In earlier chapters, a yield was chosen such as 10 per cent which, supposedly, reflected the possible growth at 5 year periods. The valuation is

Net income per annum	=	£5000
YP in perpetuity at 10 per cent	=	10
Capital value		£50 000

The same situation might be valued with a discounted cash flow allowing for a growth rate of, say, 12 per cent per annum and an equated yield of, say, 18 per cent per annum (about 2 per cent above the yield expected from undated gilt-edged stock, an 'inflation prone' investment). It has been seen earlier that single rate Years' Purchase is a summation of Present Values of £1 so that the valuation may be regarded as Table 9.1.

Table 9.1

(1) Years	(2) Income (£)	(3) Amount of £1–12 per cent	(4) Inflated Rent (£) (2 x 3)	(5) YP 5 years at 18 per cent	(6) PV at 18 per cent	(7) YP deferred at 18 per cent (5 x 6)	(8) Present Value (£) (4 x 7)
0–5	5000	1.000	5 000	3.127	1.000	3.127	15 635
5–10	5000	1.762	8 810	3.127	0.437	1.366	12 034
10–15	5000	3.106	15 530	3.127	0.191	0.597	9 271
15–20	5000	5.474	27 370	3.127	0.084	0.263	7 198
20–25	5000	9.646	48 230	3.127	0.036	0.113	5 450
25–30	5000	17.000	85 000	3.127	0.016	0.050	4 250
30–35	5000	29.960	149 800	3.127	0.007	0.022	3 295
35–40	5000	52.800	264 000	3.127	0.003	0.009	2 376
40 onwards	5000	93.051	465 255	13.333*	0.001	0.013	6 047
			Capital Value				65 556
			(say)			£65 550	

* The discounted cash flow has been terminated at 40 years, and the remaining perpetual income capitalised at an initial yield of 7½ per cent (see later explanation).

This approach has produced a capital value of £65 550 as compared with £50 000 from a traditional approach.

The 'real value' approach assumes that current inflation-proofed income will be valued at a yield reflecting real return only, i.e. an inflation risk free yield (IRFY) which may be derived from the formula

$$i = \frac{(1 + e)}{(1 + g)} - 1$$

where e = equated yield, g = growth rate (as decimals).

Thus, from above calculation,

$$i = \frac{1.18}{1.12} - 1 = 5.36 \text{ per cent}$$

An alternative method to the valuation above using the IRFY assumes that at five year intervals the purchasing power of the original £5000 per annum is restored. The valuation is still undertaken in 5 year bands but £5000 per annum is not adjusted for growth as before. Each £5000 per annum is fixed for 5 years and is inflation prone so that it is capitalised at the equated yield. The capital values obtained are in real terms not monetary terms, so that future capital values should be deferred at an inflation-proofed yield, i.e. IRFY.

Thus the valuation becomes

First 5 years as before   £15 635

5 – 10 years

Net Income per annum		£5000	
YP for 5 years at 18 per cent	3.127		
PV for 5 years at 5.36 per cent	0.77	2.408	£12 040

10 – 15 years

Net Income per annum		£5000	
YP for 5 years at 18 per cent	3.127		
PV for 10 years at 5.36 per cent	0.593	1.854	£9 270

and so on into perpetuity

It can be seen that the capital values are the same for each 5 years (apart from small 'rounding-off' discrepancies) whichever method is adopted.

Both the methods illustrated are cumbersome and a formula has been derived: namely

$$\text{Income} \times \frac{\text{YP for the review} \quad \times \quad \text{YP in perpetuity at } i \text{ per cent}}{\text{period at } e \text{ per cent}}$$

Income × YP for the review × $\dfrac{\text{YP in perpetuity at } i \text{ per cent}}{\text{YP for the review period at } i \text{ per cent}}$
           period at *e* per cent

(*e* is equated yield, *i* is IRFY)

Take the previous example,

£5000 × YP for 5 years at × $\dfrac{\text{YP in perpetuity at } 5.36 \text{ per cent}}{\text{YP for 5 years at } 5.36 \text{ per cent}}$
       18 per cent

$$£5000 \times 3.127 \times \frac{18.657}{4.291}$$

$$= £67\,980$$

This corresponds with an initial yield of approximately $7\frac{1}{2}$ per cent $\left(\text{i.e. } \dfrac{\text{Income}}{\text{Capital Value}} = \dfrac{£5\,000}{£67\,980}\right)$. This initial yield of $7\frac{1}{2}$ per cent was used for the reversion in the earlier cash flow calculation.

It is beyond the scope of this book to deal with varying freehold incomes and leasehold valuations; for further information readers are referred to the papers of Dr Ernest Wood and Neil Crosby indicated in the bibliography at the end of this chapter. (Neil Crosby in his paper proves the two formulas introduced earlier in this chapter, and also the formula following for constant rent.)

9.1.2 Constant Rent

One of the problems often emerging in the granting of a lease is the agreement of the landlord and tenant as to an appropriate rent review period. In the example in this chapter, a 5 year period has been used with an initial rent of £5000 per annum. If the review period was altered to 10 years, then the landlord would require an annual rent which would maintain this equated yield. The calculation of the revised rent would be

$$£5000 \times \frac{\text{YP for 5 years at } 'e'}{\text{YP for 5 years at } 'i'} \times \frac{\text{YP for 10 years at } 'i'}{\text{YP for 10 years at } 'e'}$$

$$= £5000 \times \frac{\text{YP for 5 years at 18 per cent}}{\text{YP for 5 years at 5.36 per cent}} \times \frac{\text{YP for 10 years at 5.36 per cent}}{\text{YP for 10 years at 18 per cent}}$$

$$= £5000 \times \frac{3.127}{4.291} \times \frac{7.593}{4.494}$$

$$= £6156 \text{ per annum}$$

9.1.3 Bibliography

Articles

Crosby N., 'The Investment Method of Valuation: A Real Value Approach', *Journal of Valuation*, Summer and Autumn 1983.
Wood Dr E., 'Positive Valuations, a Real Value Approach to Property Investments', *Estates Gazette*, vol. 226, 1973.

Tables

Bowcock P., *Property Valuation Tables*. Macmillan, 1978.
Marshall P., *Donaldsons Investment Tables*. Donaldsons, 1979.
Rose J.J., *Tables of the Constant Rent*. The Freeland Press, 1979.
Rose J.J., *Rose's Property Valuation Tables*. The Freeland Press, 1977.

Books

Baum A. and Mackmin D., *The Income Approach to Property Valuation*. Routledge & Kegan Paul, 1989.
Butler D., *Applied Valuation*. Macmillan, 1987.
Enever N., *The Valuation of Property Investments*. Estates Gazette, 1989.

10 Computer Applications

10.1 DEFINITIONS AND TERMINOLOGY

There are many definitions of the term computer. The Collins English Dictionary defines it as '... a device, usually electronic, that processes data according to a set of instructions'. The definition provided by Dixon, Hargitay and Bevan (1991) is '... a machine which under the control of a stored program, automatically accepts and processes data and supplies the results of that processing to a user'. Kirkwood (1984) offers a further variation defining a computer as '... an apparatus which accepts both numeric and textual data, processes it without user intervention, and outputs results'.

Whilst similar and broadly consistent, each of these definitions provides different insights into the nature and elements of computers. The essential ingredients that characterise a computer would seem to be: a machine, device or apparatus; a program or set of instructions; data input; processing and output. These elements and aspects of a computer are considered further below.

10.1.1 The Machine

The 'machine', 'device' or 'apparatus', generally comprises a central processing unit (CPU), display screen or visual display unit (VDU), hard and/or floppy disk drive(s), and keyboard. It may also be supported by a number of peripheral devices which include: scanner, printer and mouse. These components are collectively referred to as the computing 'hardware'. Although nowadays most of these components are generally 'electronic', it should be remembered that this need not necessarily be the case.

163

10.1.2 The Program

The 'program' is essentially the set of instructions which control and direct the computing process. A program is commonly referred to as computing 'software', and is usually stored and transferred on magnetic tape and/or floppy disk.

10.1.3 Data

The information, both textual and numeric, inputted by the user when operating a program is referred to as 'data'.

10.1.4 Processing

The processing of data is the function at the very heart of computerisation. Computers essentially fall into three categories namely 'analogue', 'digital' or 'hybrid' (a combination of analogue and digital). The operation of analogue computers requires continuous rather than discrete inputs, whereas digital computers process data in discrete units, leaving little scope for ambiguity. Digital computers are faster, and are the type generally used within the property profession.

10.1.5 Output

This is the product of computer processing. Output may be in a number of forms which include hard copy (paper printout), visual display, or output to hard or floppy disk.

10.2 COMPUTER HARDWARE

During the last twenty-five years there have been substantial developments in computer technology. The development of the *silicon chip* and the *integrated circuit* has revolutionised the manufacture and reliability of computing hardware and enabled the development of smaller, faster and more powerful machines, whilst dramatically decreasing their unit cost.

The early computers that were developed were commonly referred to as *mainframe* computers. These were generally large, cumbersome and expensive machines, operated primarily by specialist computer personnel, and requiring carefully controlled and stable operating environments.

Mainframes gained a poor reputation amongst non-specialist staff, and were suspiciously regarded as temperamental, mysterious and inaccessible. However, in more recent times this general perception of computers has changed. Nowadays, mainframes often support a network of terminals or workstations that can share information and which can be operated by non-specialist computer personnel, and are generally considered to be far more reliable, accessible, and *user-friendly*.

The technological advancements have enabled the development of the compact, self-contained, desk-top, 'personal' or 'micro' computer (PC), as an alternative to the mainframe computer. Furthermore, in more recent years, the programmable calculator and lightweight and highly portable 'lap-top' computer have been developed, further adding to the range of hardware that is available.

Such developments in hardware technology, manufacture and design have made substantial computer processing power relatively inexpensive, and readily and widely available to individuals and commercial organisations.

10.3 COMPUTER SOFTWARE

The technological advances and developments in hardware, and the availability of fast and powerful computer processing, has facilitated the development of more complex and sophisticated software.

There are many different types of computer software currently available which may be conveniently grouped into three principal categories: Programming Languages, Operating Software and Applications Software. These are briefly considered in the following sections.

10.3.1 Programming Languages

Examples of these include: Basic, Fortran, Pascal, C and Cobol. These are specially designed language systems which enable the computer programmer to input instructions to a computer in a coded form, and are used to create operating and applications software.

10.3.2 Operating Software

Examples of these include MS-DOS (Microsoft Disk Operating System), OS 2, and UNIX. Operating Software is used to control the operation of the computer hardware (including peripheral devices), and the loading of applications software.

10.3.3 Applications Software

This broad category of software may be further categorised into 'off-the-shelf' or 'speculative' software, and 'bespoke' or 'made-to-measure' software. These two groups of software are considered below.

Off-The-Shelf Software
This category of software may be further subdivided into 'Standalone' or 'General Purpose' software, and 'Application-Specific' software (Hargitay and Dixon, 1991).

(i) Standalone or General Purpose Software
These include word processor, spreadsheet, database management systems and graphics packages, as well as integrated software which combine elements of the aforementioned standalone software. In addition, expert system 'shells' are now available which provide an expert system framework from which users can develop their own expert system. The nature and use of spreadsheet packages is considered further later in this chapter in relation to property valuation and appraisal.

(ii) Application-Specific Software
This software is designed to carry out a particular single operation or range of operations. The providers of this type of software usually identify operations which might benefit from computerisation – possibly as a result of their involvement in the production of bespoke packages – and design, produce and promote off-the-shelf applications software on a speculative basis. In relation to the property profession, examples of operations for which off-the-shelf applications software are available include property management, development valuation and appraisal, and performance analysis (also refer to the following section).

Bespoke Software
This type of software is generally written to the specific design brief and requirements of an individual commissioning client, and is tailored to the precise needs of the client. It may be produced by computer programmers 'in-house', or by an external software house or computer consultant.

10.4 THE PROPERTY PROFESSIONAL AND COMPUTER APPLICATIONS

Whilst perhaps hesitant in fully embracing computer technology in the early stages of the computer revolution, many property professionals have now recognised the benefits which computers can provide in day-to-day operations as well as in strategic planning.

Software manufacturers have for some time been producing both 'bespoke' and 'off-the-shelf' applications software for a variety of property functions. These programs range from simple single function programs to complex and sophisticated multi-function packages. They encompass a range of facilities and operations which include: estate agency (including property matching and accounting); property management (records and administration); development valuation and appraisal; investment appraisal, valuation and performance measurement; zoning and general and rating valuation; property measurement and surveying; Local Government and housing association property administration; and livestock, auctions and other miscellaneous functions.

In a recent study of commercially available 'off-the-shelf' software suitable for General Practice surveying activities (The Nottingham Trent University, 1992), nearly 200 such packages were identified, available from over 90 software suppliers. With such a wide range to choose from, every General Practice property professional should be able to identify programs which will assist them in their day-to-day work.

10.5 PROPERTY VALUATION AND APPRAISAL AND COMPUTER SPREADSHEETS

10.5.1 Background and Nature of a Spreadsheet

Electronic spreadsheets first became available in the late 1970s with the introduction of VISICALC. Since then a number of rivals have been introduced which include: Supercalc, Lotus 1-2-3, Excel and Quattro Pro.

A spreadsheet is essentially a matrix of columns and rows which appear on the display screen. Each column is defined by a letter for example: A, B, C . . . AA, AB . . . BA, BB, and so on, and each row is defined by a number 1, 2, 3, etc. (VISICALC had 63 columns and 254 rows, but with more powerful machines and more sophisticated spreadsheets now available, this capacity has increased, and some spreadsheets have up to 999 columns and 9999 rows.)

The intersection of a column and a row is referred to as a 'cell', each cell having its own unique address or coordinates. For example, the cell at the intersection of column D and row 9 has the coordinate D9. It is in these cells that the user deposits data and constructs formulae (see later section).

Because of the size of a spreadsheet it is only possible for a small portion of it to appear on the display screen at any given time. A cursor (a moveable point of light) is used to identify the position on the spreadsheet. Using the four cursor control keys on the keyboard (or the mouse), the cursor may be moved up, down, left, or right on the screen, and taken to different locations on the spreadsheet. This enables the user to move about the spreadsheet and to enable different portions of it to appear on the display screen.

The computer spreadsheet provides the property analyst and valuer with a convenient, powerful and versatile tool for mathematical model-building. After only a few hours spent mastering the rudiments of a spreadsheet, it is possible for most users to produce useful working valuations and other mathematical models which can ease the computational load in many aspects of the property professionals' activities. Once saved, these models can be used time and time again, updated and further developed, making light work of repetitive mathematical operations. Investment and development valuations and appraisals – on either residual or discounted cash flow bases – are particularly suited to spreadsheets. Other examples of suitable applications include zoning and mortgage calculations, and the production of valuation and investment tables.

10.5.2 Using a Spreadsheet

Whilst modern spreadsheets provide scope for considerable sophistication which includes the construction of databases and the output of graphs, etc., it is beyond the scope of this initial introduction to consider these aspects. Having once mastered the essential elements of the spreadsheet and gained confidence in model-building, users are advised to refer directly to the user manual for their particular spreadsheet in order to further develop their spreadsheet skills.

In order to 'get going' using a spreadsheet it is necessary to master only four essential elements. These are: Data Input, Formulae Construction, Mathematical Functions and Command Functions. These elements are considered in a later section in relation to the use of

'Supercalc', although the general nature of this guidance means that it should be equally applicable to many other spreadsheets. In introducing the use of a spreadsheet it is assumed that the package has already been loaded into the computer and is ready for use.

(i) Data Input

By depositing data – be it textual or numeric – in the cells, it is possible to position numbers or text at various locations on the spreadsheet. Text is entered simply by positioning the cursor in the cell where it is intended to place the text, typing the relevant text, and pressing 'Enter' or 'Return' on the keyboard. The text should appear on the screen in the specified position. Numeric data may be entered by positioning the cursor, typing the number, and pressing 'Return' or 'Enter'. It should be noted that it is not possible to combine textual and numeric data in the same cell (although it is possible to enter numbers as text, but such entries will not be recognised by formulae).

(ii) Formulae Construction

Formulae may be constructed in cells which draw upon the numeric data entered in other cells. Having once established the formulae it is then possible to edit the original data and consider the effect that this has on the result of the calculation performed by the formulae. The great potential of this facility is that formulae representing complex mathematical relationships including a large number of numeric inputs can be created and, at the press of a button, these inputs can be changed and the effect on the end result obtained.

Formulae are constructed by using mathematical signs in conjunction with the coordinates of the cells in which the inputs are contained. Brackets ( ) are used to contain and separate elements of a formulae. The example below helps to illustrate the rudiments of formulae construction.

	A	B	C	D	E
1	1000	3000		4000	
2	20 000	14 000		6000	
3	40	50		2000	
4	16 000	2		8000	
5				8 000 000	

Data are entered in cells A1, B1, A2, B2, A3, B3, A4 and B4. In cells D1, D2, D3, D4 and D5 formulae have been constructed as follows:

Cell D1: (A1+B1)   ('+' represents addition)
Cell D2: (A2-B2)   ('−' represents subtraction)
Cell D3: (A3*B3)   ('*' represents multiplication)
Cell D4: (A4/B4)   ('/' represents division)
Cell D5: ((D1*D2) − (D3*D4))

(*Note* The use of brackets to order the elements of the calculations within the formula.)

The mathematical solutions to these formulae appear on the screen. By moving the cursor back to cell A1 and changing the data entry, the answers in cells D1 and D5 will automatically respond accordingly.

(iii) Mathematical Functions

A range of common mathematical and statistical functions are included in spreadsheet packages. These enable a variety of calculations to be performed without the need for complex manipulation of formulae. For example, if the average of the entries in cells A1, A2, A3, and A4 above is required, this can be obtained by using the average ('AV') function. If AV(A1:A4) is entered in cell A5 the answer 9260 will appear – the average of the sum of the four figures in the range A1 to A4 in the column above (note the use of the colon to denote a range). Other mathematical and statistical functions available include: summation, standard deviation, and identification of maximum and minimum figures.

(iv) Command Functions

Using the '/' key it is possible to access a range of commands which provide control over the functions and operation of the spreadsheet. These include commands for: loading and saving spreadsheet files; editing the contents of cells, formatting the layout of the screen and the presentation of the spreadsheet; and outputting the spreadsheet to a disc or printer.

10.6 EXAMPLE OF RESIDUAL VALUATION SPREADSHEET

The following example of a residual valuation spreadsheet illustrates how a spreadsheet can be used for repetitive calculations. In particular its usefulness in carrying out sensitivity analyses and/or answering 'What if?' questions in respect of possible alternative values for the input variables can be seen.

Figure 10.1 provides a printout of the spreadsheet. Textual inputs

Figure 10.1 Residual Valuation Spreadsheet

	A	B	C	D
1				
2		RESIDUAL VALUATION		
3				
4		(a) Land Acquisition Fees/Costs (%)	4	
5		(b) Site Clearance (Pounds)	0	
6		(c) GIA PSM	3500	
7		(d) ECFRV PSM GIA (Pounds)	82.50	
8		(e) ARY (%)	9.50	
9		(f) Construction Cost PSM (Pounds)	525	
10		(g) Contingencies (%)	10.00	
11		(h) QS/Arch Fees (%)	12.5	
12		(i) Finance (% PA)	12.00	
13		(j) Construction Period (Years)	1.25	
14		(k) Development Period (Years)	1.25	
15		(l) Agents/Legal Fees (%)	3.00	
16		(m) Developer's Profit (% of GDV)	12.00	
17		- -		
18				
19		Gross Development Value		
20		- - - - - - - - - - - - - - - -		
21		Gross Internal Area	3500	
22		Rent PSM	82.5	
23			- - - - - -	
24		ECFRV	288750	
25		YP in Perp at ARY	10.52632	
26			- - - - - - - - - - - - - - - - -	
27		Gross Development Value		3039474
28				
29		Less Costs:-		
30		- - - - - - -		
31		Site Clearance	0	
32		Construction	1837500	
33		Contingencies	183750	
34		QS/Architect's Fees	252656	
35		Finance	173028	
36		Agent's and Legal Costs/Fees	91184	
37		Developer's Profit	364737	
38			- - - - - -	
39				2902855
40				- - - - - - - - - - -
41		Gross Residual Value		136618
42		- -		
43				
44		Land/Site Value		
45		- - - - - - - - - - -		
46		Land/Site Value		114013
47		- -		
48		Land Acquisition Fees/Costs		4561
49		Land Finance Costs		18045
50		- -		

are contained in columns A and B. Cells C4 to C16 contain the numeric input data specified by the user. Cells C21, C22, C24, C25, C31 to C37, D27, D39, D41, D46, D48 and D49 contain formulae which draw upon the input data. The results of these formulae are displayed in the cells rather than the formulae.

If any of the input data were changed, the effect on the related calculations would be seen almost instantly, thus enabling the user to consider a range of alternative inputs and calculations very quickly.

The formulae which are contained in the spreadsheet are summarised below:

Cell	
C21:	C6
C22:	C7
C24:	C21*C22
C25:	100/C8
C31:	C5
C32:	C6*C9
C33:	(C32+C31)*(C10/100)
C34:	(C31+C32+C33)*(C11/100)
C35:	(((C31+C32+C33+C34) *((1+(C12/100))^C13)) − (C31+C32+C33+C34)/2
C36:	D27*(C15/100)
C37:	D27*(C16/100)
D27:	C24*C25
D39:	SUM(C31:C37)
D41:	D27-D39
D46:	D41/((1+C4/100)*((1+(C12/100))^C14))
D48:	D46*(C4/100)
D49:	((D46+D48)*((1+C12/100)^C14)) − (D46+D48)

(*Note* The function '^' in cells C35 and D46 is used to 'raise to the power'.)

10.7 REFERENCES

Computer Associates International *Supercalc 5, Spreadsheets, Graphics and Reporting*, 3rd edn. Computer Associates International Incorporated, 1989.

Cooke B. and Balakrishnan S.V., *Computer Spreadsheet Applications in Building and Surveying*. Macmillan Publishers Limited, 1985.

Dixon T.J., Hargitay S.E. and Bevan O.A., *Microcomputers in Property: A surveyor's guide to Lotus 1-2-3 and dBASE IV*. E. & F. N. Spon, 1991.

Feenan, R. and Dixon T.J., *Information and Technology Applications in Commercial Property*. Macmillan Press Limited, 1992.

Hargitay S. and Dixon T., *Software Selection for Surveyors*. Macmillan Publishers Limited, 1991.

Isaac D. and Steley T., *Property Valuation Techniques*. Macmillan Education Limited, 1991.

Kirkwood J., *Information Technology and Land Administration*. The Estates Gazette Limited, 1984.

The Nottingham Trent University, *Estate Surveying Software*, (Unpublished consultancy research). The Nottingham Trent University, 1992.

Answers to Questions

4.1 $i = 0.11$, $n = 1$ year, $I = £750$

$$P = \frac{I}{i \times n}$$

$$= \frac{750}{0.11 \times 1}$$

$$= £6818$$

4.2 $I = P$, $i = 0.09$

$$I = \frac{I}{P \times i}$$

$$= \frac{1}{1 \times 0.09}$$

$$= 11.11 \text{ years}$$

4.3 $P = £250$, $i = 0.095$, $n = 15$ years

$$A = P(1 + i)^n$$

$$= 250 \times 1.095^{15}$$

$$= 250 \times 3.899$$

$$= £975$$

4.4 $A = £1500$, $i = 0.085$, $n = 10$ years

$$P = \frac{A}{(1 + i)^n}$$

$$= \frac{1500}{1.085^{10}}$$

$$= \frac{1500}{2.259}$$

$$= £664$$

4.5 $A = 3P$, $n = 9$ years

$$i = \sqrt[n]{\frac{A}{P}} - 1$$

$$= \sqrt[n]{\frac{3P}{P}} - 1$$

$$= \sqrt[9]{3} - 1$$

$$= 1.13 - 1$$

$$= 0.13$$

$$= 13 \text{ per cent}$$

4.6 $S = \dfrac{n}{2}(2a + (n - 1)d)$, $a = 8$, $d = -0.25$,

$$n = \frac{8}{0.25} + 1 = 33$$

$$S = \frac{33}{2}(2 \times 8) + (32 \times -0.25)$$

$$= 16.5 \times (16 - 8)$$

$$= 16.5 \times 8$$

$$= 132$$

4.7   Let the numbers be represented by $a - d$, a, $a + d$, then

$$(a - d) + a + (a + d) = 21$$

$$3a = 21$$

$$a = 7$$

But $a(a - d)(a + d) = 280$

$$a(a^2 - d^2) = 280$$

$$7(7^2 - d^2) = 280$$

$$343 - 7d^2 = 280$$

$$7d^2 = 343 - 280$$

$$d^2 = \frac{63}{7} = 9$$

$$d = \pm 3$$

So that the numbers are 4, 7, 10

4.8 $a = 12, r = -0.5, n = 10$

$$S = \frac{a(1 - r^n)}{1 - r}$$

$$= \frac{12(1 - (-0.5^{10}))}{1 - (-0.5)}$$

$$= \frac{12 \times 0.00097}{1.5}$$

$$= \frac{12.001}{1.5}$$

$$\approx 8$$

4.9 $M = £4000, i = 0.08, n = 30$ years

$$P = \frac{M(1 + i)^n i}{(1 + i)^n - 1}$$

$$= \frac{4000 \times 1.08^{30} \times 0.08}{1.08^{30} - 1}$$

$$= \frac{4000 \times 10.05 \times 0.08}{9.05}$$

$$= \frac{3216}{9.05}$$

$$= £355$$

4.10 $P = £400$, $i = 0.09$, $n = 35$ years

$$M = \frac{P((1 + i)^n - 1)}{(1 + i)^n i}$$

$$= \frac{400 \times (1.09^{35} - 1)}{1.09^{35} \times 0.09}$$

$$= \frac{400 \times (20.37 - 1)}{20.37 \times 0.09}$$

$$= \frac{7748}{1.833}$$

$$= £4227$$

4.11 $D = £35$, $P = £1000$, $i = 0.13$

$$D = P(1 - i)^n$$

$$35 = 1000(1 - 0.13)^n$$

$$\frac{35}{1000} = 0.87^n$$

$$0.87^n = 0.035$$

$$\log 0.87 \times n = \log 0.035$$

$$n = \frac{\log 0.035}{\log 0.87}$$

$$= \frac{\bar{2}.5441}{\bar{1}.9395}$$

$$= \frac{-2 + 0.5441}{-1 + 0.9395}$$

$$= \frac{-1.4559}{-0.0605}$$

$$= 24 \text{ years}$$

4.12   For the first 3 years $P = £1200$, $i = 0.12$, $n = 3$ years

$$D = P(1 - i)^n$$

$$= 1200 (1 - 0.12)^3$$

$$= 1200 \times 0.88^3$$

$$= 1200 \times 0.6814$$

$$= £817.68$$

For the next 7 years $P = £817.68$, $i = 0.10$, $n = 7$ years

$$D = P(1 - i)^n$$

$$= 817.68 \times (1 - 0.10)^7$$

$$= 817.68 \times 0.9^7$$

$$= 817.68 \times 0.478$$

$$= £390.8$$

CHAPTER 5

5.1 $A = (1 + i)^n$

$$= 1.09^{15}$$

$$= 3.64$$

5.2 $PV = \dfrac{1}{(1 + i)^n}$

$$= \frac{1}{1.075^{14}} = \frac{1}{2.752}$$

$$= 0.3633$$

5.3   Net income per annum $= £150$

YP for 8 years at $8\frac{1}{2}$ per cent

$$YP = \frac{1 - \dfrac{1}{(1 + i)^n}}{i}$$

$$= \frac{1 - \dfrac{1}{1.085^8}}{0.085}$$

$$= \frac{1 - \dfrac{1}{1.92}}{0.085}$$

$$= \frac{0.4792}{0.085} \qquad = \underline{5.63}$$

Capital value = £844

5.4   £250

$$s = \frac{i}{A - 1}$$

$$= \frac{0.06}{1.06^{16} - 1}$$

$$= \frac{0.06}{2.54 - 1}$$

$$= \frac{0.06}{1.54} \qquad = \underline{0.0389}$$

£9.725

5.5 Net income per annum = £225

YP in perpetuity
deferred 5 years at
8 per cent   =

$$\frac{1}{iA} = \frac{1}{0.08 \times 1.08^5}$$

$$= \frac{1}{0.08 \times 1.469}$$

$$= \frac{1}{0.1175} \qquad = \underline{8.51}$$

Capital value = £1915

5.6 Staircase repair   £200
PV of £1 for 5 years
at 6 per cent

$$= \frac{1}{(1 + i)^n} = \frac{1}{1.06^5}$$

$$= \frac{1}{1.339} = \underline{0.747}$$

$$\text{£}149$$

Roof repairs $\qquad$ £500

PV of £1 for 8 years
at 6 per cent

$$= \frac{1}{(1 + i)^n} = \frac{1}{1.06^8}$$

$$= \frac{1}{1.593} = \underline{0.627}$$

$$\underline{\text{£}313}$$

$$\text{Present liability} = \text{£}462$$

5.7

$$\text{YP} = \frac{1}{i + s\left(\dfrac{1}{1 - x}\right)}$$

$$= \frac{1}{0.09 + \left(\dfrac{0.03}{1.03^{15} - 1} \times \dfrac{1}{1 - 33/100}\right)}$$

$$= \frac{1}{0.09 + \left(0.0537 \times \dfrac{1}{0.67}\right)}$$

$$= \frac{1}{0.09 + 0.0801}$$

$$= \frac{1}{0.1701}$$

$$= 5.878$$

5.8   Net income per annum = £500

YP for 25 years at 10 per cent
and 5 per cent gross (tax 33p
in £)

Net interest = Gross X $(1 - x)$

$$= 5 \times 0.67 \approx 3\tfrac{1}{2} \text{ per cent}$$

$$YP = \cfrac{1}{i + s\left(\cfrac{1}{1 - x}\right)}$$

$$= \cfrac{1}{0.10 + \left(\cfrac{0.035}{1.035^{25} - 1} \times \cfrac{1}{0.67}\right)}$$

$$= \cfrac{1}{0.10 + \left(0.0256 \times \cfrac{1}{0.67}\right)}$$

$$= \cfrac{1}{0.10 + 0.0382}$$

$$= \cfrac{1}{0.1382} = \qquad \underline{7.236}$$

Capital value $= £3618$

5.9

$$YP = \cfrac{1}{i + s\left(\cfrac{1}{1 - x}\right)}$$

$$8 = \cfrac{1}{i + \left(\cfrac{0.025}{1.025^{32} - 1} \times \cfrac{1}{0.6}\right)}$$

$$8 = \cfrac{1}{i + \left(0.0207 \times \cfrac{1}{0.6}\right)}$$

$$8 = \cfrac{1}{i + 0.0345}$$

$$8\,(i + 0.0345) = 1$$

$$i = \frac{1 - (8 \times 0.0345)}{8}$$

$$= \frac{1 - 0.276}{8} = \frac{0.724}{8}$$

$$= 0.09$$

$$= 9 \text{ per cent}$$

5.10 (i) Net income per annum = £750

YP for 19 years at 7 per cent and

$2\frac{1}{2}$ per cent net

$$= \frac{1}{i + s} = \frac{1}{0.07 + \dfrac{0.025}{1.025^{19} - 1}}$$

$$= \frac{1}{0.07 + 0.0417} = \frac{1}{0.1117}$$

$$= \underline{8.95}$$

Capital value = £6712

(ii) Net income per annum = £750

YP for 19 years at 7 per cent and

$2\frac{1}{2}$ per cent net (tax 40p in £)

$$= \frac{1}{i + s\left(\dfrac{1}{1 - x}\right)} = \frac{1}{0.07 + \left(0.0417 \times \dfrac{1}{0.6}\right)}$$

$$= \frac{1}{0.07 + 0.0695}$$

$$= \frac{1}{0.1395} \qquad = \underline{7.16}$$

Capital value = £5370

5.11   £12 300 × (i + s)

$$= £12\,300 \times \left(0.08 + \frac{0.025}{1.025^{10} - 1}\right)$$

$$= £12\,300 \times (0.08 + 0.0892)$$

$$= £12\,300 \times 0.1692$$

$$= £2081$$

5.12 Monthly repayment $= 20 \times \dfrac{(i + s)\ 100}{12}$

$$= [20 \times \left(0.085 + \dfrac{0.085}{1.085^{20} - 1}\right) \times 100]/12$$

$$= \dfrac{20 \times (0.085 + 0.0206) \times 100}{12}$$

$$= \dfrac{20 \times 0.1056 \times 100}{12}$$

$$= £17.6$$

5.13 Let borrowing amount (in 100 £s) $= x$

$$25 = \dfrac{x \times (i + s)\ 100}{12}$$

$$25 = [x \times \left(0.095 + \dfrac{0.095}{1.095^{18} - 1}\right) \times 100]/12$$

$$25 = x \times \dfrac{(0.095 + 0.023) \times 100}{12}$$

$$25 = x \times \dfrac{0.118 \times 100}{12}$$

$$25 = x \times 0.99$$

$$x = \dfrac{25}{0.99} = 25.25$$

Hence maximum amount $= £2525$ (that is, 25.25×100)

5.14 Given that the Amount of £1 per annum in 10 years at 10 per cent $= 15.937$ and $(1.10)^9 = 2.358$

Amount of £1 p.a. $= \dfrac{A - 1}{i}$

So that $15.937 = \dfrac{A - 1}{0.10}$

A for 10 years at 10 per cent $= (15.937 \times 0.10) + 1$

$$= 2.5937$$

A for 9 years at 10 per cent = 2.358

But *A* for 19 years at 10 per cent = *A* for 10 years × *A* for 9 years

$$= 2.5937 \times 2.358$$

$$= 6.116$$

But PV of £1 = 1/*A* so that

PV of £1 for 19 years at 10 per cent

$$= \frac{1}{6.116}$$

$$= 0.1635$$

5.15 Given that the Years' Purchase of a reversion to a perpetuity at 10 per cent after 19 years is 1.635, this is

YP in perpetuity × PV of £1 in 19 years
at 10 per cent   at 10 per cent

So that $1.635 = \dfrac{1}{i} \times \dfrac{1}{A}$

$$1.635 = \frac{1}{0.1A}$$

$$A = \frac{1}{0.1635} = 6.116$$

A for 19 years at 10 per cent = 6.116

A for 20 years at 10 per cent = *A* for 19 years × *A* for 1 year

$$= 6.116 \times (1 + i) = 6.116 \times 1.10 = 6.727$$

But *s* for 20 years at 10 per cent $= \dfrac{i}{A - 1} = \dfrac{0.10}{6.727 - 1}$

$$= \frac{0.10}{5.727}$$

$$= 0.01746$$

5.16 YP in perpetuity at 10 per cent deferred 24 years is 1.0. This is

YP in perpetuity × PV of £1 in 24 years at 10 per cent

$$1.0 = \frac{1}{i} = \frac{1}{A}$$

$$1.0 = \frac{1}{0.1A}$$

So that $A = 10$

$$\text{Amount of £1 per annum} = \frac{A - 1}{i} = \frac{10 - 1}{0.1}$$

$$= 90$$

Amount of £1 per annum for 24 years at 10
per cent = 90

5.17 Amount of £1 per annum in 6 years at 7 per cent = 7.153.
This is

$$7.153 = \frac{A - 1}{i}$$

$$7.153 = \frac{A - 1}{0.07}$$

$$A = 7.153(0.07) + 1 = 1.501$$

Hence the Amount of £1 for 6 years at 7 per cent = 1.501 and
the Amount of £1 for 5 years at 7 per cent $(1.07)^5$ is given as
1.403. The Amount of £1 for 11 years at 7 per cent

$$= A \text{ for 6 years} \times A \text{ for 5 years}$$

$$= 1.501 \times 1.403$$

$$= 2.106$$

But PV of £1 for 11 years at 7 per cent

$$= \frac{1}{A} = \frac{1}{2.106}$$

$$= 0.4749$$

5.18 PV of £1 in 15 years at 6 per cent = 0.4173

$$A = \frac{1}{PV} = \frac{1}{0.4173} = 2.4$$

Amount of £1 for 15 years at 6 per cent = 2.4, but

$$s = \frac{i}{A - 1} = \frac{0.06}{2.41 - 1} = 0.043$$

Annual Sinking fund to produce £1 in 47 years at 5 per cent = 0.0055

5.19 (i) PV of £1 in 47 years at 5 per cent = 0.1, but

$$A = \frac{1}{PV} = \frac{1}{0.1} = 10$$

Amount of £1 of 47 years at 5 per cent = 10, but

$$s = \frac{i}{A - 1} = \frac{0.05}{10 - 1} = 0.0055$$

Annual Sinking fund to produce £1 in 47 years at 5 per cent = 0.0055

(ii) Present Value of £1 p.a. $= \dfrac{1 - PV}{i}$

$$= \frac{1 - 0.1}{0.05} = 18$$

Present Value of £1 p.a. in 47 years at 5 per cent = 18

5.20 Amount of £1 per annum in 10 years at 4 per cent = 12; *s* is the reciprocal of this

$$s = \frac{1}{12} = 0.0833$$

Years' Purchase for 10 years at 8 per cent and 4 per cent net (tax 50p in £) =

$$= \frac{1}{i + s\left(\dfrac{1}{1-x}\right)}$$

$$= \frac{1}{0.08 + 0.0833\left(\dfrac{1}{1-0.5}\right)}$$

$$= \frac{1}{0.08 + (0.0833 \times 2)} = \frac{1}{0.08 + 0.1666}$$

$$= \frac{1}{0.2466} = 4.005$$

Years' Purchase for 10 years at 8 per cent and 4 per cent net (tax 50p in £) = 4.055

5.21 PV of £1 in 30 years at $5\frac{1}{2}$ per cent = 0.20; but Amount of £1 = 1/PV

$$A \text{ for 30 years at } 5\tfrac{1}{2} \text{ per cent} = \frac{1}{0.20} = 5$$

$$s = \frac{i}{A - 1}$$

So that s for 30 years at $5\frac{1}{2}$ per cent =

$$\frac{0.055}{5 - 1} = \frac{0.055}{4}$$

$$= 0.0138$$

5.22 PV of £1 in 11 years at 7 per cent = 0.475

$$\text{Present Value of £1 per annum} = \frac{1 - PV}{i}$$

So that Present Value of £1 per annum in 11 years at 7 per cent

$$= \frac{1 - 0.475}{0.07} = \frac{0.525}{0.07}$$

$$= 7.5$$

5.23 Years' Purchase in 20 years at $7\frac{3}{4}$ per cent $= 10.0$

$$10 = \frac{1 - PV}{i}$$

$$10 = \frac{1 - PV}{0.0775}$$

$$PV = 1 - (10 \times 0.0775)$$

$$= 1 - 0.775$$

$$= 0.225$$

PV of £1 in 20 years at $7\frac{3}{4}$ per cent $= 0.225$

$$A \text{ for 20 years at } 7\frac{3}{4} \text{ per cent} = \frac{1}{PV} = \frac{1}{0.225}$$

$$= 4.444$$

Amount of £1 per annum in 20 years at $7\frac{3}{4}$ per cent

$$= \frac{A - 1}{i} = \frac{4.444 - 1}{0.0775} = \frac{3.444}{0.0775}$$

$$= 44.44$$

5.24 Present Value of £y in 8 years at 10 per cent $= x$ so that PV of £1 in 8 years at 10 per cent $= x/y$ but Amount of £1 is the reciprocal of PV of £1; hence

Amount of £1 in 8 years at 10 per cent $= \frac{y}{x}$

Amount of £1 per annum $= \frac{A - 1}{i}$

Amount of £1 per annum in 8 years at 10 per cent

$$= \frac{\dfrac{y}{x} - 1}{0.10}$$

$$= 10\left(\frac{y}{x} - 1\right)$$

5.25 £330 represents the capital value of the right to receive £100 per annum for 6 years deferred by a period of 7 years at a 6 per cent return. This may be shown as follows

Net income per annum   £100

Amount of £1 per annum × PV of £1

$$\frac{A - 1}{i} \times \frac{1}{A}$$

$$= \frac{1 - \dfrac{1}{A}}{i} \quad \text{which is}$$

YP for 6 years at 6 per cent

$$= \frac{1 - \dfrac{1}{(1.06)^6}}{0.06} = \frac{1 - \dfrac{1}{1.418}}{0.06}$$

$$= \frac{1 - 0.705}{0.06} = \frac{0.295}{0.06} = 4.9$$

This YP of 4.9 has then been deferred by multiplying it by the PV of £1; Hence 3.3 is the YP for 6 years deferred 7 years at 6 per cent, that is, 100 × 3.3 = £330, which is the value of £100 per annum for 6 years deferred 7 years at 6 per cent.

5.26 3.337 is the value of the right to receive £1 per annum for 5 years but deferred 4 years at 6 per cent. This could be calculated as follows

YP for 5 years at 6 per cent × PV of £1 for 4 years at 6 per cent

$$= \frac{1 - \dfrac{1}{A} \times \dfrac{1}{A}}{i}$$

$$= \frac{1 - \dfrac{1}{1.06^5} \times \dfrac{1}{1.06^4}}{0.06}$$

$$= \frac{1 - \dfrac{1}{1.338} \times \dfrac{1}{1.2625}}{0.06}$$

$$= \frac{1 - 0.747}{0.06} \times 0.792$$

$$= \frac{0.253 \times 0.792}{0.06} = 3.339$$

(slight difference due to 'rounding off')

5.27 Reduce 4 per cent gross to a net rate

$$4 \times \frac{1 - x}{1}$$

$$= 4 \times \frac{1 - 0.25}{1} = 4 \times 0.75$$

$$= 3 \text{ per cent net}$$

A YP of 10 has been paid for 25 years of income

$$YP = \frac{1}{i + s\left(\dfrac{1}{1 - x}\right)}$$

$$10 = \frac{1}{i + \left(\dfrac{0.03}{1.03^{25} - 1} \times \dfrac{1}{0.75}\right)}$$

$$10 = \frac{1}{i + \left(0.0274 \times \frac{1}{0.75}\right)}$$

$$10 = \frac{1}{i + 0.0365}$$

$$i = \frac{1 - 0.365}{10} = \frac{0.635}{10} = 0.0635$$

$$= 6.35 \text{ per cent}$$

5.28 £1 at the end of each year for 10 years at 10 per cent

$$= \frac{A - 1}{i} = \frac{1.10^{10} - 1}{0.10}$$

$$= \frac{2.594 - 1}{0.10}$$

$$= 15.94$$

If it is assumed that this is left for the next 10 years at 10 per cent it would accumulate to

$$15.94 \times (1 + i)^n$$

$$= 15.94 \times 1.10^{10}$$

$$= 15.94 \times 2.594 = \qquad 41.35$$

£2 at the end of each year for 10 years at 10 per cent

$$= 2 \times \frac{A - 1}{i}$$

$$= 2 \times 15.94 \text{ (already calculated) } \underline{31.88}$$

$$\text{Result} = £73.23$$

5.29 Let s = sinking fund for the first 5 years at $2\frac{1}{2}$ per cent. In 5 years, s would accumulate to

$$s \times \frac{A - 1}{i}$$

$$= s \times \frac{1.025^5 - 1}{0.025}$$

$$= s \times 5.256 = 5.256s$$

If this accumulates for a further 5 years, it will accumulate to

$$5.256s \times (1 + i)^n$$

$$= 5.256s \times 1.025^5$$

$$= 5.256s \times 1.1314 = 5.946s$$

The sinking fund for the next 5 years is $2s$. This will accumulate to

$$2s \times \frac{A - 1}{i}$$

$$= 2s \times 5.256 \text{ (as before)} = 10.512s$$

The total accumulation is $16.458s$ which equals £1000, so that

$$s = \frac{1000}{16.458} = £60.76$$

Annual amount for first 5 years = £60.76

5.30 Let s = sinking fund for the first 5 years at 5 per cent. In 5 years s would accumulate to

$$s \times \frac{A - 1}{i}$$

$$= s \times \frac{1.05^5 - 1}{0.05}$$

$$= s \times 5.5256 = 5.5256s$$

If this accumulates for a further 5 years, it will accumulate to

$$5.5256s \times (1 + i)^n$$

$$= 5.5256s \times 1.05^5$$

$$= 5.5256s \times 1.276 = 7.05s$$

The sinking fund for the next 5 years is 2s. This will accumulate to

$$2s \times \frac{A - 1}{i}$$

$= 2s \times 5.5256$ (as before) $= 11.05s$

The total accumulation is 18.10s which equals £22 630, so that

$$s = \frac{22\ 630}{18.10} = £1250$$

Annual amount for first 5 years = £1250, and for second 5 years = £2500

5.31 Amount of £1 for 9 years at 8 per cent = £2. For 10 years

$$A = 2 \times (1 + i)$$
$$= 2 \times 1.08 = 2.16$$

Sinking fund for 10 years at 8 per cent

$$= \frac{i}{A - 1} = \frac{0.08}{2.16 - 1}$$

$$= \frac{0.08}{1.16}$$

$$= 0.0689$$

Monthly repayment to redeem £5000 in 10 years at 8 per cent =

$$\frac{5000\ (i + s)}{12} = \frac{5000\ (0.08 + 0.0689)}{12}$$

$$= \frac{5000 \times 0.1489}{12}$$

$$= £62.04$$

5.32 Annual sinking fund in 10 years at 6 per cent = 0.07587

Annual repayment to redeem to £3000 in 10 years at 6 per cent

$= 3000 \ (i + s)$

$= 3000 \ (0.06 + 0.07587)$

$= 3000 \times 0.13587$

$= £407.61$

Capital outstanding after 9 years = Annual repayment × YP for unexpired term

$= 407.61 \times$ YP for 1 year at 6 per cent

$$= 407.61 \times \frac{1}{i + s} = \frac{1}{0.06 + \dfrac{0.06}{1.06 - 1}}$$

$$= 407.61 \times \frac{1}{0.06 + 1}$$

$$= 407.61 \times \frac{1}{1.06}$$

$= £384.54$

5.33 (i) Profit rent per annum $= £2000$

$$YP = \frac{1}{i + s} = \frac{1}{0.10 + \dfrac{.03}{1.03^5 - 1}}$$

$$= \frac{1}{0.10 + 0.1884} = \frac{1}{0.2884} = \underline{3.467}$$

Capital value $= £6934$

(ii) 10 per cent remunerative return on £6934 = £693.4. Balance of profit rent is sinking fund contribution, i.e. £2000 − £693.4 = £1306.6. If £1306.6 per annum is invested at 3 per cent for 5 years, it will accumulate to:

£1306.6 × Amount of £1 per annum for 5 years at 3 per cent =

$$£1306.6 \times \frac{A - 1}{i}$$

$$= \pounds1306.6 \times \frac{1.03^5 - 1}{0.03}$$

$$= \pounds1306.6 \times 5.309 = \pounds6936$$

(£2 difference due to 'rounding-off' figures.)

5.34 (i) Outlay	= £7580	
Plus 10 per cent	= £758	
		£8338
Less Income – Year 1	= £2000	
		£6338
Plus 10 per cent	= £633.8	
		£6971.8
Less Income – Year 2	= £2000	
		£4971.8
Plus 10 per cent	= £497.18	
		£5468.98
Less Income – Year 3	= £2000	
		£3468.98
Plus 10 per cent	= £346.90	
		£3815.88
Less Income – Year 4	= £2000	
		£1815.88
Plus 10 per cent	= £181.59	
		£1997.47
Less Income – Year 5	= £2000	
Balance		– £2.53

(Balance should be zero, difference due to 'rounding-off' figures.)

(ii) Outlay is £7580 – 10 per cent return gives £758 per annum.

(iii) Balance of £2000 – £758 is £1242 per annum. This is the annual sinking fund, which if invested at 10 per cent per annum for 5 years, will accumulate to:

£1242 × Amount of £1 per annum for 5 years at 10 per cent =

$$\pounds1242 \times \frac{A - 1}{i} =$$

$$£1242 \times \frac{1.10^5 - 1}{0.10} =$$

£1242 × 6.105 = £7582

(£2 difference due to 'rounding off' figures.)

CHAPTER 6

6.1 Discounted Inflow

£10 000 × PV of £1 for 1 year at 9 per cent = 0.917 = £9170
£11 000 × PV of £1 for 2 years at 9 per cent = 0.842 = £9262
£12 000 × PV of £1 for 3 years at 9 per cent = 0.772 = £9264
£13 000 × PV of £1 for 4 years at 9 per cent = 0.708 = £9204
+ £36 900

NPV = £36 900 − £36 000 = +£900

To find IRR, assume target rate of 11 per cent.
Discounted Inflow

£10 000 × PV of £1 for 1 year at 11 per cent = 0.901 = £9010
£11 000 × PV of £1 for 2 years at 11 per cent = 0.812 = £8932
£12 000 × PV of £1 for 3 years at 11 per cent = 0.732 = £8784
£13 000 × PV of £1 for 4 years at 11 per cent = 0.659 = £8567
+£35 293

NPV = −£36 000 + £35 293 = −£707

By similar triangles

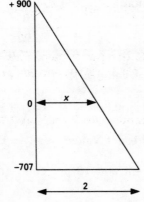

$$\frac{x}{900} = \frac{2}{1607}$$

$$x = \frac{1800}{1607} = 1.12$$

IRR = 9 + 1.12 = 10.12 per cent

6.2   Assume a target rate of 7 per cent, and calculate the Net Present Value.

Net income per annum	=	£15 000
YP for 2 years at 7 per cent	=	<u>1.808</u>
		£27 120

Reversion

Net rack rental value per annum	=	£20 000
YP in perpetuity deferred 2 years at 7 per cent	=	<u>12.478</u>
	=	<u>£249 560</u>
Capital value	=	£276 680
Less Initial outlay	=	<u>£213 500</u>
Net Present Value	=	+£63 180

The target rate of 7 per cent gives a Net Present Value of +£63 180; re-calculate the valuation, using a target rate of say 10 per cent.

Net income per annum	=	£15 000
YP for 2 years at 10 per cent	=	<u>1.735</u>
	=	£26 025

Reversion

Net rack rental value per annum	=	£20 000
YP in perpetuity deferred 2 years at 10 per cent	=	<u>8.264</u>
	=	<u>£165 280</u>
Capital value	=	£191 305
Less Initial outlay	=	<u>£213 500</u>
Net Present Value	=	−£22 195

The IRR must lie between 7 per cent and 10 per cent, and may be found by similar triangles.

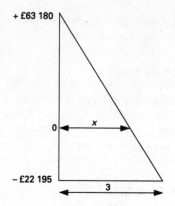

Let the base line of the triangle = difference between the two target rates, i.e. $10 - 7 = 3$; the height of the triangle = total value of NPVs (ignoring signs); $x =$ IRR − lower rate of interest.

$$\text{Then } \frac{x}{63\,180} = \frac{3}{85\,375}$$

$$x = \frac{3 \times 63\,180}{85\,375} = 2.22$$

IRR = $7 + 2.22$ = say 9 1/4 per cent

6.3 Calculation of rent at each rent review:

First 5 years   £20 000 per annum

Second 5 years £20 000 × Amount of
£1 for 5 years at 5 per cent =
£20 000 × 1.2763 = £25 526 per annum

Third 5 years £20 000 × Amount of
£1 for 10 years at 5 per cent =
£20 000 × 1.6289 = £32 578 per annum

Fourth 5 years £20 000 × Amount of
£1 for 15 years at 5 per cent =
£20 000 × 2.0789 = £41 578 per annum

Fifth 5 years £20 000 × Amount of
£1 for 20 years at 5 per cent =
£20 000 × 2.6533 = £53 066 per annum

Sixth 5 years   £20 000 × Amount of
£1 for 25 years at 5 per cent =
£20 000 × 3.3864 = £67 728 per annum

(*Note* The rent for each review is calculated by increasing
£20 000 per annum with compound interest at 5 per cent per
annum, i.e £20 000 × Amount of £1 for *n* years at 5 per cent.)

Assume a target rate of 8 per cent, and calculate the Net
Present Value.

Net income per annum	=	£20 000
YP for 5 years at 8 per cent	=	3.993
	=	£79 860

Net income per annum	=	£25 526
YP for 5 years at 8 per cent	=	3.993
PV of £1 in 5 years at 8 per cent	=	0.68
YP for 5 years at 8 per cent deferred 5 years	=	2.715
	=	£69 303

Net income per annum	=	£32 578
YP for 5 years at 8 per cent	=	3.993
PV of £1 in 10 years at 8 per cent	=	0.463
YP for 5 years at 8 per cent deferred 10 years	=	1.849
	=	£60 237

Net income per annum	=	£41 578
YP for 5 years at 8 per cent	=	3.993
PV of £1 in 15 years at 8 per cent	=	0.315

YP for 5 years at 8 per cent deferred 15 years	=	<u>1.258</u>
	=	£52 305

Net income per annum	=	£53 066
YP for 5 years at 8 per cent	=	3.993
PV of £1 in 20 years at 8 per cent	=	<u>0.214</u>
YP for 5 years at 8 per cent deferred 20 years	=	<u>0.854</u>
	=	£45 318

Net income per annum	=	£67 728
YP for 5 years at 8 per cent	=	3.993
PV of £1 in 25 years at 8 per cent	=	<u>0.146</u>
YP for 5 years at 8 per cent deferred 25 years	=	<u>0.583</u>
	=	£39 485

Residue	=	£200 000
PV of £1 in 30 years at 8 per cent		<u>0.099</u>
	=	<u>£19 800</u>

Capital value	=	£366 308
Less Initial outlay	=	<u>£322 500</u>
Net Present Value	=	+£43 808

The target rate of 8 per cent gives a Net Present Value of +£43 808; re-calculate the valuation using a target rate of 10 per cent.

Net income per annum	=	£20 000
YP for 5 years at 10 per cent	=	<u>3.791</u>
	=	£75 820

Net income per annum   =   £25 526

YP for 5 years at 10 per cent   =   3.791

Pv of £1 in 5 years at 10 per
    cent   =   0.621

YP for 5 years at 10 per cent
    deferred 5 years   =   2.354

                                  =   £60 088

Net income per annum   =   £32 578

YP for 5 years at 10 per cent   =   3.791

PV of £1 in 10 years at 10 per
    cent   =   0.386

YP for 5 years at 10 per cent
    deferred 10 years   =   1.463

                                  =   £47 662

Net income per annum   =   £41 578

YP for 5 years at 10 per cent   =   3.791

PV of £1 in 15 years at 10 per
    cent   =   0.239

YP for 5 years at 10 per cent
    deferred 15 years   =   0.906

                                  =   £37 670

Net income per annum   =   £53 066

YP for 5 years at 10 per cent   =   3.791

PV of £1 in 20 years at 10 per
    cent   =   0.149

YP for 5 years at 10 per cent
    deferred 20 years   =   0.565

                                  =   £29 982

Net income per annum   =   £67 728

YP for 5 years at 10 per cent   =   3.791

PV of £1 in 25 years at 10 per
    cent   =   <u>0.092</u>

YP for 5 years at 10 per cent
    deferred 25 years   =   <u>0.349</u>

                                       =   £23 637

Residue   = £200 000

PV of £1 in 30 years at 10 per
    cent   =   <u>0.057</u>

                                       =   <u>£11 400</u>

            Capital value   =   £286 259

       Less Initial outlay   =   <u>£322 500</u>

        Net Present Value   =   −£36 241

The IRR must lie between 8 per cent and 10 per cent, and may
be found by similar triangles.

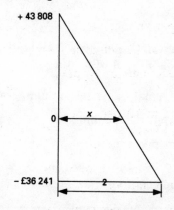

Let the base line of the triangle = difference between the two
target rates i.e. 10 − 8 = 2; the height of the triangle = total
value of NPVs (ignoring signs); x = IRR − lower rate of interest.

$$\text{Then } \frac{x}{43\ 808} = \frac{2}{80\ 049}$$

$$x = \frac{2 \times 43\ 808}{80\ 049} = 1.094$$

IRR = 8 + 1.094 = (say) 9 per cent.

CHAPTER 7

7.1 (i) *Freehold interest.* Assuming a freehold yield for a ground rent with long term fixed income is 20 per cent, and for the office building is 8 per cent.

Ground rent per annum	=	£750
YP for 49 years at 20 per cent	=	<u>4.999</u>
		£3749

Reversion

Net rack rental value per annum	=	£25 000
YP in perpetuity deferred 49 years at 8 per cent	=	<u>0.288</u>
		<u>£7200</u>

Capital value	=	<u>£10 949</u>
(say)	=	£10 950

Leasehold interest. Assuming a leasehold yield of 9 per cent and a tax liability of 30p in £.

Net rack rental value per annum	=	£25 000
Less Ground rent per annum	=	£ <u>750</u>
Profit rent per annum	=	£24 250
YP for 49 years at 9 per cent and 2½ per cent net (tax 30p in £)	=	<u>9.508</u>

Capital value	=	<u>£230 569</u>
(say)	=	£230 550

(ii) *Value of unencumbered freehold.*

Net rack rental value per annum	=	£25 000
YP in perpetuity at 8 per cent	=	<u>12.5</u>
		£312 500

Less Freehold interest	=	£10 950
Leasehold interest	=	£230 550
	=	£241 500
Marriage gain	=	£ 71 000

7.2

X's interest

Assuming a freehold yield of 7 per cent for shop premises.

Unexpired term of lease is 7 years

Rent received per annum	=	£5000
YP for 7 years at 15 per cent	=	4.16
		£20 800

Reversion

Net rack rental value per annum = £12 000		
YP in perpetuity deferred 7 years at 7 per cent	=	8.896
	=	£106 752
Capital value	=	£127 552
(say)	=	£127 550

(*Note* The premium of £3000 was paid 14 years ago, and has no relevance to the calculation of capital value at the present time.)

Y's interest

Assuming a leasehold yield of 8 per cent and a tax liability of 30p in £.

Unexpired term of sublease is 3 years

Rent received per annum	=	£7000
Less Rent paid per annum = £5000		
External repairs and insurance say 12½ per		

cent of net rack
rent £12 000   = £1500   = £6500

Net income per annum   = £ 500

YP for 3 years at 8 per cent
and $2\frac{1}{2}$ per cent net (tax
30p in £)   = 1.837   £ 918

Remaining 4 years

Net rack rental value per annum = £12 000

Less Rent paid per annum   = £ 5000

Profit rent per annum   = £ 7000

YP for 4 years at 8 per cent
and $2\frac{1}{2}$ per cent net (tax
30p in £)   = 2.358

PV of £1 in 3 years
at 8 per cent   = 0.794

YP for 4 years at 8 per cent
and $2\frac{1}{2}$ per cent net (tax 30p
in £) deferred 3
years   = 1.872

                                           £13 104

            Capital value   = £14 022

                (say)   £14 000

(*Note* The premium of £4000 was paid 11 years ago, and has no relevance to the calculation of capital value at the present time.)

Z's interest

Assuming a subleasehold yield at 9 per cent and a tax liability of 30p in £.

Adjusted rack rental value per annum =

Net rack rental value per annum +
external repairs and insurance =
            £12 000 + £1500   = £13 500

Less Rent paid per annum	=	£7000
Profit rent per annum	=	£6500

YP for 3 years at 9 per cent and $2\frac{1}{2}$ per cent net (tax 30p in £)	=	1.804

Capital value	=	£11 726
(say)		£11 750

7.3
A's interest

Assuming a freehold yield for a ground rent with long term fixed income is 20 per cent, and for the office building is 8 per cent.

Ground rent per annum	=	£1000	
YP for 65 years at 20 per cent	=	5	£5000

Reversion

Net rack rental value per annum	=	£8000	
YP in perpetuity deferred 65 years at 8 per cent	=	0.084	£ 672

Capital value	=	£5672
(say)		£5650

B's interest

Assuming a leasehold yield of 9 per cent, and a tax liability of 30p in £.

Unexpired term of sublease is 14 years

Rent received per annum		=	£4000
Less Rent paid per annum	= £1000		
External repairs and insurance say $12\frac{1}{2}$ per cent of net rack rent – £8000	= £1000	=	£2000
Net income per annum		=	£2000

YP for 14 years at 9 per cent
and $2\frac{1}{2}$ per cent net (tax 30p
in £)   = <u>5.666</u>

                                        £11 332

Remaining 51 years

Net rack rental value per annum = £8000

Less Rent paid per annum   = £<u>1000</u>

Net income per annum   = £7000

YP for 51 years at 9 per cent
and $2\frac{1}{2}$ per cent net (tax 30p
in £)   = 9.601

PV of £1 in 14 years at
9 per cent   = <u>0.299</u>

YP for 51 years at 9 per
cent and $2\frac{1}{2}$ per cent net
(tax 30p in £) deferred
14 years   = <u>2.87</u>

                                        £<u>20 090</u>

Capital value   = £<u>31 422</u>

(say)   = £31 400

C's interest

Assuming a subleasehold yield of 10 per cent and a tax liability of 30p in £.

Unexpired term of sublease is 2 years

Rent received per annum   = £6000

Less Rent paid per annum   = £4000

Internal repairs say 5
per cent of net rack
rent £8000   = £<u>400</u>   = £<u>4400</u>

Net income per annum   = £1600
YP for 2 years at 10 per cent and
$2\frac{1}{2}$ per cent net (tax 30p in £)   = <u>1.242</u>

£1987

Remaining 12 years

Rack rental value on internal
repairing terms = Net rack rental
value + external repairs and
insurance = £8000 + £1000   = £9000

Less Rent paid per annum   = £<u>4000</u>

Net income per annum   = £5000
YP for 12 years at 10 per
cent and $2\frac{1}{2}$ per cent net
(tax 30p in £)   = 4.913

PV of £1 in 2 years
at 10 per cent   = <u>0.826</u>

YP for 12 years at 10 per cent
and $2\frac{1}{2}$ per cent net (tax 30p
in £) deferred 2 years   = <u>4.058</u>

     = <u>£20 290</u>

Capital value   = <u>£22 277</u>

(say)   = £22 300

D's interest

Assuming a subleasehold yield of 10 per cent, and a tax liability of 30p in £.

Rack rental value per annum where there is no liability for repairs
= Net rack rental value +
all repairs and insurance =
£8000 + £1000 + £400   = £ 9400

Less Rent paid per annum   = £ <u>6000</u>

Profit rent per annum   = £ 3400

YP for 2 years at 10 per cent

and $2\frac{1}{2}$ per cent net (tax 30p
in £)   = <u>1.242</u>

Capital value   = £ <u>4222</u>

(say)   = £ 4200

7.4   *Freehold interest.* Assuming a freehold yield of 8 per cent.

Unexpired term of lease is 16 years

Rent received per annum   = £ 7000

YP for 16 years at 15 per cent   = <u>5.954</u>

£41 678

Reversion

Net rack rental value per annum = £12 000

YP in perpetuity deferred 16
years at 8 per cent   = <u>3.649</u>

£43 788

Plus Premiums   = £7000

PV of £1 in 2 years at 8
per cent   = <u>0.857</u>

£5999

= £7000

PV of £1 in 9 years at 8
per cent   = <u>0.5</u>

<u>£3500</u>

£94 965

Less Surface water drain   = £3000

PV of £1 in 2 years at $2\frac{1}{2}$
per cent   = <u>0.952</u>

£<u>2856</u>

Capital value   = £<u>92 109</u>

(say)   = £92 100

Leasehold interest. Assuming a leasehold yield of 9 per cent and a tax liability of 30p in £.

Net rack rental value per annum	= £12 000	
Less Rent paid per annum	= £ <u>7000</u>	
Profit rent per annum	= £ 5000	
YP for 16 years at 9 per cent and $2\frac{1}{2}$ per cent net (tax 30p in £)	= <u>6.108</u>	
		= £30 540

Less Premiums	= £7000		
PV of £1 in 2 years at $2\frac{1}{2}$ per cent	= <u>0.952</u>		
	= £7000	£6664	
PV of £1 in 9 years at $2\frac{1}{2}$ per cent	= <u>0.8</u>		
		£5600	
			£12 264
Capital value		=	£18 276
(say)		=	£18 300

7.5 *Freehold interest.*
Assuming a freehold yield of 8 per cent for a small office block.

Rental value last year = 4 × £9000 = £36 000 per annum.

(*Note* It is assumed that last year's letting of £9000 per annum was at full rental value = 25 per cent of total value.)

Current net rack rental value	= £36 000 +
$5\frac{1}{2}$ per cent (£1980)	= £37 980 per annum

Period to rent review is 1 year

Rent received per annum	= £30 000	
YP for 1 year at 15 per cent	= 0.87	
		£26 100

Rent review

Net rack rental value per annum	= £37 980	
YP in perpetuity deferred 1 year at 8 per cent	= 11.574	
		£439 580
Capital value	= £465 680	
(say)	£465 700	

Leasehold interest.

Assuming a leasehold yield of 8 per cent and a tax liability of 30p in £. Yield reflects 16 years of further occupation, although there is currently only one year's profit rent to be valued.

Net rack rental value per annum of retained portion – 75 per cent of £37 980	= £28 485	
Plus Rent per annum from sublessee	= £ 9000	
Total income per annum	= £37 485	
Less Rent paid per annum	= £30 000	
Net income per annum	= £ 7485	
YP for 1 year at 8 per cent and $2\frac{1}{2}$ per cent net (tax 30p in £)	= 0.663	
Capital value	= £4963	
(say)	£4950	

Subleasehold interest.

Assuming a subleasehold yield of 8 per cent and tax liability of 30p in £. Yield reflects 16 years of further occupation, although there is currently only one year's profit rent to be valued.

Net rack rental value per annum	= £9495
Less Rent paid per annum	= £9000
Profit rent per annum	= £ 495

YP 1 year at 8 per cent and
$2\frac{1}{2}$ per cent net (tax 30p
in £) 0.663

Capital value	= £328
(say)	£350

7.6 (i) *Traditional method*

Profit rent per annum	= £3000

YP for 4 years at 8 per cent
and $2\frac{1}{2}$ per cent net
(tax 30p in £) = 2.358

£7074

Profit rent per annum	= £5000

YP for 4 years at 8 per cent
and $2\frac{1}{2}$ per cent net (tax
30p in £) = 2.358

PV of £1 in 4 years
8 per cent = 0.735

YP for 4 years at 8 per cent
and $2\frac{1}{2}$ per cent net (tax
30p in £) deferred 4 years = 1.733

£8665

Capital value	= £15 739
(say)	= £15 750

(ii) *Double Sinking Fund Method*

Let capital value = *x*

Profit rent per annum	= £3000

Less Annual sinking fund to replace
x in 8 years at $2\frac{1}{2}$
per cent net   = 0.114x

Adjusted for tax
at 30 per cent   = <u>1.428</u>   <u>0.163x</u>

Spendable income per annum = £3000 − 0.163x

YP for 4 years at 8 per cent = <u>3.312</u>

                                £9936 − 0.54x

Remaining 4 years
Profit rent per annum   = £5000

Less Annual sinking fund as before = <u>0.163x</u>

Spendable income per annum = £5000 - 0.163x
YP for 4 years at 8
per cent   = 3.312

PV of £1 in 4 years
at 8 per cent = <u>0.735</u>

YP for 4 years at 8 per cent
deferred 4 years   = <u>2.434</u>

                                <u>£12 170 − 0.397x</u>
                                £22 106 − 0.937x

Plus

Repayment of capital replaced by
single rate sinking fund = x

PV of £1 in 8 years at 8
per cent = $\dfrac{0.54}{\text{Capital value}}$ = $\dfrac{0.54x}{£22\ 106 − 0.397x}$

But capital value = x

$x = £22\ 106 − 0.397x$

$1.397x = £22\ 106$

$x = \dfrac{22\ 106}{1.397}$

    = £15 824

(iii) *Pannell's Method*

Profit rent per annum	=	£3000
YP for 4 years at 8 per cent	=	3.312

$$£9936$$

Profit rent per annum	=	£5000

YP for 4 years at 8 per cent	= 3.312	
PV of £1 in 4 years at 8 per cent	= 0.735	
YP for 4 years at 8 per cent deferred 4 years	= 2.434	£12 170
Capital value on single rate basis	= £22 106	

$$\text{Annual equivalent} = \frac{£22\ 106}{\text{YP for 8 years at 8 per cent}}$$

$$= \frac{22\ 106}{5.7466} = £3847 \text{ per annum}$$

Constant rent per annum	=	£3847
YP for 8 years at 8 per cent and $2\frac{1}{2}$ per cent net (tax 30p in £)	=	4.106
Capital value	=	£15 796

(iv) *Sinking Fund Method*

Let capital value = x

Spendable income = $0.08x$

Profit rent per annum = £3000

$$\textit{Less} \text{ Spendable income per annum} = \frac{0.08x}{£3000 - 0.08x}$$

$$\textit{Less} \text{ Tax at 30 per cent} = \frac{900 - 0.024x}{£2100 - 0.056x}$$

   × Amount of £1 per annum
for 4 years at $2\frac{1}{2}$ per cent
             = 4.1525
× Amount of £1 for 4
years at $2\frac{1}{2}$ per cent
             = <u>1.1038</u>   <u>4.584</u>

                      £9626 − 0.2567x

Profit rent per annum	= £5000
Less Spendable income per annum	= $\dfrac{0.08x}{}$
	£5000 − 0.08x
Less Tax at 30 per cent	= £1500 − 0.024x

                      £3500 − 0.056x

× Amount of £1 per annum
for 4 years at $2\frac{1}{2}$ per cent   = <u>4.1525</u>
                     = <u>£14 534 − 0.2325x</u>

          Capital value = £24 160 − 0.4892x

But capital value = x

x = £24 160 − 0.4892x

x = $\dfrac{24\,160}{1.4892}$

x = £16 223

CHAPTER 8

8.1 Analyse the recent sale to obtain the yield applicable to the income obtainable from the first review onwards.

Term to the first rent review is 2 years

Rent received per annum	=	£30 000
YP for 2 years at 15 per cent	=	<u>1.626</u>

                                £48 780

First Rent Review

> Net rack rental value per annum = £40 000
>
> YP in perpetuity deferred
>
> > 2 years at i $\qquad \underline{\quad x \quad}$

$$\underline{£40\,000x}$$

> Capital value (given) $= £477\,500$

Therefore, £477 500 = £48 780 + £40 000x

$$x = \frac{477\,500 - 48\,780}{40\,000}$$

$$= 10.718$$

YP in perpetuity deferred 2 years at i = 10.718

Using *Parry's Valuation and Investment Tables.*

Look up the Years' Purchase of a Reversion to a perpetuity table across the 2 year line, the nearest YP figure to 10.718 is 10.717, i.e. a yield of 8 per cent. Applying these results:

Net rack rental value for the whole office block is £50 000 per annum.
Ratio of upper floors to ground floor is 1.5:1, ie values of £30 000 and £20 000 per annum respectively.

Freehold interest

Assuming a freehold yield of 8 per cent.

Ground floor

> Net rack rental value per annum = £20 000
>
> YP in perpetuity at 8 per cent $= \underline{\quad 12.5 \quad}$

$$£250\,000$$

Upper floors
Unexpired term of lease is 3 years

	Rent received per annum	=	£24 000
Less	External repairs and insurance say $12\frac{1}{2}$ per cent of net rack rent − £30 000	=	£3750
	Net income per annum	=	£20 250
	YP for 3 years at 15 per cent	=	2.283
			£46 231

Reversion

Net rack rental value per annum	=	£30 000
YP in perpetuity deferred 3 years at 8 per cent	=	9.923
		£297 690
		343 921
Capital value	=	593 921
(say)	=	£593 950

Leasehold interest

Assuming a yield of 9 per cent and a tax liability of 30p in £.

Adjusted rack rental value per annum =

Net rack rental value per annum + external repairs and insurance = £30 000 + £3750 = £33 750.

Adjusted rack rental value per annum   = £33 750

Less Rent paid per annum	=	£24 000
Profit rent per annum	=	£ 9750
YP for 3 years at 9 per cent and $2\frac{1}{2}$ per cent net (tax 30p in £)	=	1.804
Capital value	=	£17 589
(say)	=	£17 600

8.2 Analysing the rent of £72 500 per annum: assume that the depth of the shop is split from the front into two 6.10 m zones, leaving a balance of 4.80 m. The value of the second zone is assumed to be 50 per cent of the front zone and the rear zone 50 per cent of the second zone. If the rent per square metre of the front zone is assumed to be £x, the rental value will be

front zone – zone A   7 m × 6.10 m × x = 42.7x

second zone – zone B 7 m × 6.10 m × 0.5x = 21.35x

rear zone – remainder 7 m × 4.80 m × 0.25x = 8.4x

 72.45x

$$72.45x = £72\ 500$$

$$x = \frac{£72\ 500}{72.45} = £1000/m^2\ ITZA$$

Analysis of freehold sale:

$$Yield = \frac{Rental\ Value}{Capital\ Value} = \frac{72\ 500}{1\ 035\ 500}$$

$$= 0.07,\ i.e.\ 7\ per\ cent.$$

Adopting the principles used in the analysis, the annual rental value of the second shop will be

zone A – 6 m   × 6.10 m × £1000 = £36 600

zone B – 6 m   × 6.10 m × £ 500 = £18 300

remainder – 6m × 7.80 m × £ 250 = £11 700

 Annual rental value   = £66 600

Valuation

Freehold interest

Term to the first rent review is 3 years

Rent received per annum	= £60 000
Less External repairs and insurance say 12½ per cent of net rack rent £66 600	= £ 8325
Net income per annum	= £51 675
YP for 3 years at 15 per cent =	2.283
	£117 974

Reversion

Net rack rental value per annum	= £66 600
YP in perpetuity deferred 3 years at 7 per cent	= £11.661
	= £776 623
Capital value	= £894 597
(say)	= £894 600

Leasehold interest

Assuming a yield of 8 per cent and a tax liability of 30p in £.

Adjusted rack rental value per annum = Net rack rental value + external repairs and insurance = £66 600 + £8325	
	= £74 925
Less Rent paid per annum	= £60 000
Profit rent per annum	= £14 925
YP for 3 years at 8 per cent and 2½ per cent net (tax 30p in £)	= 1.837

$$\text{Capital value} = \underline{£27\,417}$$
$$\text{(say)} = £27\,400$$

8.3 Total site coverage = 7000 m² × 40 per cent = 2800 m² gross external area.

Reducing 2800 m² by 10 per cent gives 2520 m² net internal area.

10 per cent – offices 252 m²

90 per cent – production area 2268 m².

Assumptions

Rents – Offices £90/m²

Production area £50/m²

Yield 7 per cent

Building cost £400/m² (gross)

Building period 2 years

Valuation

Offices	– 252 m² × £90	=	£22 680
Production area	– 2268 m² × £50	=	£113 400
			£136 080

YP in perpetuity at 7 per cent   <u>14.28</u>

Gross Development Value   £1 943 222

Less

Site preparation, say = £10 000

Cost of building 2800 m² × £400/m² = £1 120 000

Contingencies say 10 per cent = £113 000

Architects' and quantity surveyors' fees, say 10 per

cent of cost and
contingencies   =   £124 300

Financing – 2 years at
12 per cent on $\frac{1}{2}$ of £1 367 300
= $(1.12^2 \times £683\,650)$ –
£683 650   =   £173 920

Legal costs, advertisement
and estate agency fees, say 3 per
cent of value   =   £58 297

Developer's profit say 10 per
    cent of value   =   £194 322

                                           1 793 839

        Residue   =   149 383

This residue represents the value of land x, acquisition costs say 4 per cent of value, and the cost of borrowing for 2 years at 12 per cent per annum on land value and costs

Residue £149 383 = $1.04x \times 1.12^2$

£149 383 = $1.3046x$

Site value = $\dfrac{£149\,383}{1.3046}$ = £114 505

(say)   £114 500

Index

Access of light 19
Accounts method 151, 152
Accumulative rate of interest 73, 75, 77, 132
Action area plans 21
Advertisements 20, 21, 22
Agricultural Holdings Act 1948 16
Agricultural land 16, 29, 37, 42, 110, 146
Agriculture (Maintenance, Repair and Insurance of Fixed Equipment) Regulations 1973 37
Air conditioning 25
Airports 26
All risks yield 157
Amount of £1 58, 59, 60, 62, 63, 70, 72, 85, 86, 87, 89, 94, 125, 128, 129, 158, 184, 185, 186, 187, 188, 189, 192, 194, 199, 200, 216
Amount of £1 per annum 61, 62, 63, 85, 86, 87, 92, 93, 125, 126, 128, 129, 184, 185, 186, 187, 189, 190, 195, 196, 216
Analogue 164
Annual equivalent 80, 127, 130, 131, 132, 215
Annual Sinking Fund 57, 63, 64, 65, 72, 73, 77, 78, 81, 82, 84, 85, 88, 92, 93, 96, 120, 121, 126, 127, 128, 130, 132, 143, 187, 188, 193, 194, 196, 214, 215
Annuity £1 will purchase,
  dual rate 80, 131
  single rate 81, 82
Arithmetical progressions 43, 45, 56
Assets Valuations Standards Committee 4
Assign 16
Assignee 16
Assignment 16
Auction 2, 89, 93

Bad debts 35
Bank of England 10
Bank rate 10
Banks 3, 9, 10, 11
'Bar the entail' 18
Baum, A. and Mackmin, D. 161
Baum, A. and Sams G. 137
Big Bang 12
Bingo hall 25
Boarding houses 23
Boilers 34, 38
Bonds 13
Bowcock, P. 8, 94, 161
Broiler houses 153
Building controls 22–24
Building preservation notice 22
Building Regulations 1991 22
Building society(ies) 3, 9, 10, 11
Buildings of special architectural or historic interest 22
Business tenancies 16
Butler, D. 155, 161

Capital Gains Tax 6
Capital value 2, 8, 31, 67, 68, 69, 70, 71, 72, 73, 74, 75, 76, 77, 78, 79, 80, 82, 90, 94, 107, 108, 109, 110, 112, 114, 117, 119, 120, 121, 123, 126, 127, 128, 129, 134, 135, 138, 140, 145, 148, 149, 151, 152, 153, 158, 159, 180, 182, 183, 195, 198, 201, 204, 206, 207, 208, 209, 210, 212, 213, 214, 215, 216, 217, 218, 219, 220, 221
Caravan site 23
Caravan Sites Act 1968 24
Caravan Sites and Control of Development Act 1960 23
Carpeting 35
Cell 168, 169, 170

Central area shops 39
Central heating 25
Central Processing Unit 163
Change of use 21, 22
Changes in legislation 26
Changes in taste and demand 25
Characteristic 43
Characteristics of land and
    property 36–42
Charities 120
Cinema 22, 25, 41, 151, 152
Cleanliness 23
Clearance areas 23
Coal-mining 26
Code of Measuring Practice 147
Colleges 153
Commercial property 27, 28, 29, 36
Common difference 43, 45
Common ratio 45, 46
Comparison method 29, 145–9
Compound Interest 50–2, 55
Compulsory purchase 21
Computer 57, 163
Confectionery shop 22
Conservation areas 22
Constant rent 128, 160, 161, 215
Contingencies 149, 151, 221
Contractor's method 153–5
Controls on land usage 18–22
Costs construction
  and site works 149, 150
  estate agency and advertising 149,
    150
Costs of transactions 28
Council Tax 36
Crematoria 26
Crosby N. 160, 161
Cursor 168

Databases 168
Data input 163, 169
Debenture stocks 13
Decentralisation 26
Decoration 25
Defective Premises Act 1972 23, 33,
    34
Defence Bonds 12
Deferred income 109, 118
Deferred value 60
Deposit account 9
Depreciation 54, 55, 56
Depreciated Replacement Cost 154,
    155
Deterioration of the structure 25
Developer(s) 149

Developer's profit 149, 150, 222
Development, definition of 21
Development land 149, 151
Development Land Tax 6
Development plans 26
Digital 164
Director General of Fair Trading 7
Disability allowance 153
Discounted cash flow 99–105
Dividend 13, 14
Dominant tenement 19, 20
Double Sinking Fund 126, 127, 129,
    143, 213
Drinking water 23
Dual rate tables 57, 73–81
Duty of care 23, 33
Dwelling houses 38

Easements 18, 19, 20
Economic activities 26
Effect of adjacent activities 26
Electricity substations 26
Enever, N. 161
Equated yield 157
Equitable interests 17
Equities 12
Estate agent 2
European Union 10, 38
Exclusive rent 36
Express grant 19
External influences 24, 25

Face value 12
Factories Act 1961 23, 41
Factory(ies) 23, 33, 41, 142, 147
Factory inspector 23
Fairgrounds 151
Farm buildings 37
Fee simple absolute in possession 16
Fees
  architect's 149, 150, 221
  estate agency 149, 150, 222
  legal 149, 150, 222
  quantity surveyor's 149, 150, 222
Fencing 18
Fire 24, 34
  means of escape in case of 23, 41
  warning of 23
Fire fighting 23
Fire insurance 155
Fire Precautions Act 1971 23
First-aid facilities 23
Fixed-interest securities 12, 13, 27
Flats 34, 38
Flooding 24, 34

Food takeaways 25
Freehold 16, 17, 18, 67, 101, 104, 105, 108
Freehold interests, valuation of 107–16
Freeholder 16, 24, 36
Full repairing and insuring lease 117, 131, 144, 155
Full repairing and insuring terms 108, 109, 110, 113, 114, 143
Further education establishment 26

General improvement areas 23
General rates 36
Geometrical progressions 45–7, 62
Gilts 12, 113
Gipsies 24
Government department 4
Gross adjustment factor 78, 121
Gross development value 149, 221
Gross value 153
Ground rent 36, 135, 136, 204, 207

Hard core or layer method 114–16
Hard/floppy disk drives 163, 164
Hardware 163
Head lease 17
Head lessee 16, 17, 141
Head rent 17
Heating 41
High-rise buildings 41
Highways 22
Horizontal slicing 115
Hostilities 24
Hotels 23, 41, 151, 152
House(s) 23
Housing Acts 1957–85 16, 23
Housing associations 38
Hybrid 164
Hypermarkets 39

Ideal investment 9, 24
Implied grant 19
Improvement grants 23
Inclusive rent 36
Income tax 6
Incorporated Society of Valuers and Auctioneers 1, 147
Industrial estate 26
Industrial group 4
Industrial premises 41, 42
Inflation 27, 37, 61, 109, 157
Inflation prone 113, 135, 157
Inflation risk free yield 157, 158, 159
Inheritance Tax 4

Initial yield 103, 104, 157
Inland Revenue 36
Insanitary houses 23
Institutional investors 37
Institution,
  for research 23
  for teaching 23
  for training 23
  providing treatment or care 23
Insurance 4, 24, 33, 38, 123
Insurance company(ies) 3, 153
Insurance group 4
Integrated circuit 164
Internal rate of return 81, 100–5, 197–9, 203
Internal repairing lease 17, 124, 135, 144
Internal repairing terms 17, 123, 142
Internal repairs 17
Intervals less than one year 70, 71
Intervals more than one year 71, 72
Investment 9
Investment market 9
Investment method 145
Investor 9, 24, 26, 27, 28, 50, 55
ITZA 143, 144, 219

Joint stock companies 12

Keyboard 163, 168

Land economist 2
Landlord 3, 16, 17, 23, 25, 27, 32, 33, 34, 37, 66
Landlord and Tenant Act 1954 3, 16
Landlord's services 34
Lands Tribunal 7, 18, 151, 154, 155
Law of Property Act 1925 15
Law of Property Act 1969 3
Lease 16, 29, 31, 33, 108
  full repairing and insuring 17, 31, 34
  ground 17, 36, 37, 112
  head 17
  internal repairing 17, 108, 133, 155
  sub- 117
Leasehold 73, 90, 117, 118, 119, 120, 137
Leasehold interests, valuation of 116–22
Leasehold Reform Act 1967 16
Leasehold Reform, Housing and Urban Development Act 1993 16, 38
Leaseholder 16

Leasing 24, 25
Legal estate(s) 5, 15
Legislation, changes in 26, 67
Lessee 16, 29, 36, 129, 130, 137
Lessor 29
Licences 18
Lift systems 25
Lifts 34, 38
Lightning damage 24
Listed buildings 22
Local authority 6, 12, 22, 23, 36, 38
Local government 4
Local Government, Planning and Land
    Act 1980 21
Local Government Act 1985 21
Local government loans 13
Local planning authority(ies) 6, 26
Local plans 21
Local shops 39
Long user 19
Lost modern grant 20

Machine 163
Mainframes 164, 165
Management 34, 108
Management of traffic 21
Market value 14
Marginal Income 115, 116
Marriage value 137–41
Marshall, P. 8, 161
Mathematical functions 170
Minerals 1, 41
Minimum lending rate 10
Monthly tenancies 34
Mortgage(s) 4, 11, 52, 53, 54, 94
Mortgage instalment table 57, 82–4
Mortgagee 52
Mortgagor 52, 54
Motorways 26
Mouse 163
Museums 154

National House-building Council
    scheme 23
National Savings Bank 11
National Savings Certificates 11
Nationalised industry 4
Net adjustment factor 77
Net income 68, 69, 70, 74, 75, 76,
    76, 77, 80, 81, 88, 90, 102, 103,
    107, 108, 117, 118, 120, 121,
    134, 136, 140, 145, 158, 159,
    179, 180, 181, 183, 190, 198,
    200, 201, 206, 207, 208, 209,
    212, 218, 220

Net present value 99, 197–9, 201,
    202, 203
Net rack rental value *see* Rack rental
    value
Nominal value 13
Non-tax-paying investors 120–2
Nottingham Trent University 167, 173

Occupation lease 17
Occupation rent 17
Office(s) 25, 33, 34, 40, 41, 42, 108,
    118, 141, 142, 155, 221
Offices, Shops and Railway Premises
    Act 1963 23, 40
Oil refineries 154
Oral agreement 17
Ordinary shares 13
Outgoings 31
Output 163, 164
Overcrowding 23
Overdraft 11

Pannell's Method 126, 127, 129, 143,
    215
Parry's *Valuation and Investment
    Tables* 8, 94, 103, 148, 217
Patterns of yields 42
Pension funds 15
Peppercorn rent 37
Perpetual income 108
Personal computer 165
Personal loan 11
Personal occupation 24
Physical life 25
Places of entertainment 23
Planned maintenance programme 32
Planning and Compensation Act
    1991 21
Planning (Listed Buildings and
    Conservation Areas) Act 1990 22
Planning control 6, 20–2
Planning permission 22
Porterage 38
Porters 34
Power stations 154
Preference shares 13
Premium 25, 29, 34, 93, 129–32,
    142, 153, 205, 210, 211
Prescription 19
Prescription Act 1832 19, 20
Present Value of £1 60, 61, 63, 65,
    66, 68, 69, 71, 72, 84, 85, 86,
    87, 89, 93, 99, 107, 110, 116,
    125, 132, 158, 159, 180, 181,
    185, 186, 187, 188, 189, 190,

191, 200, 201, 202, 203, 206, 207, 208, 209, 211, 213, 214, 215
Present Value of £1 per annum (dual rate) 73–81
Present Value of £1 per annum (single rate) 65–68
Printer 163, 166
Private control 18
Private negotiation 2
Profit rent 117, 119, 122–4, 125, 126, 127, 128, 129, 130, 135, 136, 143, 149, 195, 209, 211, 213, 214, 215, 216, 217, 219
Profits *à prendre* 18, 19, 20
Profits method 151, 152
Program 164
Programming languages 165
Property bonds 15
Property company 4
Property Misdescriptions Act 1991 7
Property Owner's Liability Policy 34
Public highway 20
Public houses 25, 151
Purchaser with a Special Interest 4, 5, 137–41

Quantity surveyor 149, 150

Rack rent 17
Rack rental value 29, 30, 33, 34, 36, 101, 105, 108, 109, 110, 111, 112, 113, 114, 115, 119, 120, 122, 124, 131, 133, 135, 136, 140, 141, 147, 148, 155, 198, 204, 206, 207, 208, 209, 210, 211, 212, 213, 217, 220
Railway premises 23
Railway stations 26
Rateable value 36, 153
Rates 3, 36
Rating 4
Real property 15
Real rate of interest 93
Real value 26, 157
Regional shopping centres 39
Reinstatement cost 34
Reinstatement method 152, 153,
Remunerative rate of interest 75, 132, 152
Rent 7, 24, 27, 29, 30, 31, 35, 76
  exclusive 36
  ground 17, 112, 113
  head 17
  inclusive 36
  net rack *see* Rack Rental Value

occupation 32
peppercorn 37
profit 17
Rent Acts 1965–77 16
Rent as a percentage of turnover 27
Rental factor 104
Rent Charges Act 1977 35
Rent charges 35
Rent reviews 3, 27, 108
Rental value 28
  determination of 28, 29
Repairs 32
  methods of estimation 32–3
Reserve price 3
Residential property(ies) 26, 33, 36, 38
Residual method 149–51
Restrictive covenants 18
Reversion 69, 102, 109, 112, 113, 114, 125, 134, 135, 204, 205
Reversionary income 113
Rights of light 19
Rights of way 19
Roof repairs 72, 180
Rose, J.J. 8, 94, 161
Royal Institution of Chartered Surveyors 1, 4, 147, 154

Safety 22
Sanitary accommodation 41
Sanitary conveniences 22
Scanner 163
Schools 23
Secretary of State for National Heritage 22
Secretary of State for Home Affairs 23
Security 9
Service charges 3, 142
Servient tenement 19
Settled Land Act 1925 18
Sewage-disposal works 153
Sewage-treatment works 26
Sewerage rates 36
Shop(s) 7, 29, 30, 33, 42, 67, 90, 101, 104, 113, 117, 130, 133, 141, 146, 155, 219
  central area 39
  confectionery 22
  local 39
  self-service unit 39
  suburban 39
Shopping unit 39
Silicon chip 164
Simple interest 47–9, 55
Single Rate tables 57–73

Sinking fund *see* Annual Sinking Fund
Sinking fund method 128, 129
Site licence 24
Software 165, 166, 167
Sole trader 39
Speculation 5
Speculators 5, 6
Spendable income 73, 74, 76, 80,
　　125, 126, 127, 128, 129, 214,
　　215, 216
Sporting rights 41
Spread sheets 167, 169, 170
Staircase 63, 72, 180
Standard amenities 23
Statements of Asset Valuation Practice
　　and Guidance Notes 154
Statute 19
Statutory controls 20
Stock Exchange 11, 12, 13
Stock Exchange Automated Quotation
　　System 12
Stocks and shares 11, 12, 13
Structure plans 21
Subleasehold 16, 117, 119, 134, 136
Sublessee 16, 122, 134
Sublessor 16
Sublet 16
Subsidence 24
Suburban shops 39
Supercalc 169, 172
Surface water drain 142, 210

Target rate of interest 99, 101, 104
Tax on sinking fund 77–80
Taxation 4
Tenancy agreement 17, 31
Tenancy for life 17
Tenancy in fee simple 16
Tenancy in fee tail 17
Tenant 16, 25, 28, 33, 66
Tenant for life 17
Tender 2
Term certain 16
Terms of years absolute in
　　possession 16
Theatres 22, 41, 151
Town and country planning 2
Town and Country Planning Act
　　1947 20
Town and Country Planning Act
　　1968 20
Town and Country Planning Act
　　1971 20
Town and Country Planning Act
　　1990 20

Town and Country Planning (Use
　　Classes Order) 1987 21
Town halls 153
Town plans 21
Tree preservation orders 22
Trunk roads 26
Turf accountant's office 22

Underlessee 16
Underlessor 16
Uniform Business Rate 36
Unit of comparison 29
Unit trusts 13
Unitary Development Plans 21
Universities 92
Urban estate manager 2

Valuation, definition of 2
　　methods of 145–53
Valuation formulae, interrelationship
　　of 84–94
Valuation Officer 36
Valuation tables 7, 8, 59, 62
　　construction and analysis of 57–97
Value Added Tax 152
Valuer, function of the 2
Vandalism 24, 34
Varying income 109, 118
Ventilation 23, 41
Vertical Slicing 115
Video hire shop 25
Village plans 21
Visicalc 167
Visual Display Unit 163
Voids 35

Warehouses 33, 41
Washing facilities 23
Water rates 36
Wayleaves 18
Weekly tenancies 34
Wood, E. 160, 161

Years' Purchase 8, 31, 83, 107, 145,
　　151
Years' Purchase (dual rate) 73–81, 87,
　　88, 91, 96, 116, 122, 125, 130,
　　134, 140, 141, 149, 181, 182,
　　183, 188, 192, 204, 206, 207,
　　208, 209, 211, 213, 219, 220
Years' Purchase in perpetuity 67, 68,
　　92, 95, 108, 115, 116, 135, 158,
　　185, 204, 221
Years' Purchase of a reversion to a
　　perpetuity 68, 69, 92, 102, 107,

109, 115, 135, 146, 158, 159,
180, 198, 204, 205, 210, 212,
217, 218, 220
Years' Purchase (single rate)   65–8,
76, 84, 87, 94, 95, 107, 140, 158,
159, 179, 189, 195, 198, 200,
201, 202, 203, 204, 205, 210,
212, 216, 218, 220

Yield(s)   9, 13, 14, 25, 30, 37, 38,
40, 42, 81, 82, 108, 114, 119,
122, 124, 133, 143, 145, 147,
148, 149, 157, 158, 159, 160,
197–206, 211, 219, 221

Zoning method   146, 147, 219